To the Undiscovered Ends

So glad you enjoyed the book,
and that it gave you a few
laughs.
My best wishes
Kathleen.

To the Undiscovered Ends

Kathleen Upton

The Pentland Press Limited
Edinburgh · Cambridge · Durham

First published in 1992 by
The Pentland Press Ltd.
5 Hutton Close
South Church
Bishop Auckland
Durham

ISBN 1   85821   001   1

Typeset by Elite Typesetting Techniques,
Southampton.
Printed and bound by Antony Rowe Ltd.,
Chippenham.

To Ron
with love and thanks
for all his support

to Konny
who encouraged me to write

and to all the people
whose lives touched ours
and who are part of my story

Contents

Chapter 1

Reasons

'What about Australia?'

'What about Australia?' I must have sounded stupid, echoing my husband's question, but after yet another sleepless night I wasn't feeling bright.

I have often thought how one chance remark can alter the course of one's life, but that one question certainly altered ours. It was Coronation Week in 1953, bleak, wet and utterly miserable. More like November than June, and we felt as miserable as the weather.

Ron was a fireman on the railway and the steam trains were being phased out in favour of diesel engines, thus making firemen redundant. He had taken a post at Three Bridges to learn to drive the engines, but we were unable to find anywhere to live. We had no money for a deposit on a house, even if one had been available, and there were no flats or houses to rent. Later there would be plenty as Crawley was about to be extended. Crawley was one of the so-called New Towns and council accommodation would be allocated to any family working within the area.

The hours Ron worked were long and mostly the late shift. When his shift was finished, he was too late for a train back to St. Leonards, so he would lie down in a railway carriage in a siding, snatch a few hours sleep and catch the first train home in the morning. We would have a few hours together, a meal, then he would be off again until the next morning.

It was a very disjointed kind of life and with Vivienne, our small daughter, suffering badly from asthma, we felt increasingly despondent. Most nights were disturbed with her coughing and vomiting and it was quite usual to have to change her bedding two or three times during the night.

1

Our basement flat was damp, had one bedroom and no bathroom, but we were low on the housing list as we were 'adequately housed' according to the council officials. We had tried every remedy for asthma suggested by doctors, friends and relatives, and each evening lit a herbal lamp in the bedroom, to no avail, the only effect being to make the flat smell like a permanent compost heap. It had been almost two years since we had enjoyed an unbroken night's sleep. During our last visit to the child specialist at our local hospital, he had asked if it was possible for us to go abroad to work for a couple of years as he felt our daughter's condition would probably improve in a warmer climate. We had discussed it, but it had not seemed a practical solution. And then Ron's question, 'What about Australia?'

'Do you mean emigrate?'

'Why not? What have we got to lose? We have no chance of housing in Three Bridges in the near future, we don't know if my job will be permanent; if we did consider it, now is the time. I could go up to Australia House on my next rest day and find out more about it.'

I looked around at the wet bed linen draped across the kitchen and thought of the low wages we tried to manage on, the food still on ration and said, 'Well, why not?'

The next week he went to London and brought back all the colourful brochures of the various states, booklets explaining the rules and conditions of the government in power at the time, the medical services and so on. All the pictures depicted endless sunshine, blue skies, white sandy beaches, surf riders and bikini-clad girls. Paradise!

We pored over them. 'Can you imagine never being cold again?' I said. 'Or going into a shop and buying a dozen eggs, or a joint of meat?' We were very short of food still; in fact we saved all our meat rations for four weeks and then bought a whole joint, not very big. The other three weeks we ate horse meat: a shop in Silverhill sold only horse meat for human consumption and it was quite tasty. We had extra cheese rations as Ron was in an occupation where a canteen was not available. The twelve ounces a week were, in theory, supposed to be used in his sandwiches, but in practice we had to make three dinners from it. The prospect of unlimited food was a dream, and the thought of warm weather for most of the year, where fuel would be a minor problem, enticing.

'Well, what do you think? All we have to do is fill in the forms and find a sponsor. That shouldn't be too difficult.' Ron was over-optimistic. If we were acceptable, passed our medicals and could find a sponsor who would guarantee us a place to live, it would be plain sailing.

We began to ask around our friends if they knew of anyone living out there who might be a suitable sponsor. We collected quite a number of addresses, someone in every state except the Northern Territory. I wrote a dozen or more letters, posted them and sat back to await results. In our first flush of enthusiasm, we had imagined it would be easy.

The replies were so disappointing. We didn't actually know any of the people to whom we wrote, but according to our informants, they were all 'doing very well'. Some didn't answer at all, some just wrote to say that they had booked their passage home, having served their two years. This was the minimum stay if you went out under the 'Assisted Scheme', whereby it cost ten pounds per person. If you didn't stay two years, however, you had to pay back to the government the full cost of the journey out as well as your fare home, which latter you had to pay in any case. So it was very unusual for anyone to come home before the two years had elapsed.

Several of the replies were so guarded in tone that we were wondering if it was such a good idea after all, when a letter arrived from Queensland that raised our hopes again.

It was from an Englishwoman who had been out there about five years, and loved it. She wrote in glowing terms of the beauty of the district in which she and her family lived, the tropical fruits in the garden, the rolling Pacific Ocean, only yards distant, the easy way of life and so on. Utopia had nothing on that particular patch of Queensland!

'Doesn't it sound idyllic?' It was November by now, the flat was damper than usual and the summer had been wet and cold. I could almost smell the frangipani in her garden.

'She says they can find us a small flat quite easily and there is plenty of work in Brisbane,' Ron said. 'I don't mind what I do.'

So we were half-way there. He gave up his job on the railway and took a temporary job as a builder's labourer, hod carrying or concrete work, until we had progressed from form filling to medical examinations, X-rays and eventually the all-important interview with the official who would make the final decision on our suitability.

It was late November when we were asked to go to the Labour Exchange in Hastings where prospective emigrants were interviewed. The day came and Vivienne was so ill that it was impossible to take her out. We asked a neighbour to sit with her while we attended, only to be told that all members of the family must be seen. So it was arranged that Mr Foster, who was the official from Australia House, would come to our flat in the evening. He was an enormous man, with a brown leathery face and a harsh accent. He stood in our doorway, filling the aperture.

'Good day.' His eyes scanned the room quickly. We felt he wasn't missing a thing.

'So this is the child.' He went to sit beside her, asking all sorts of questions, many of which did not seem relevant, and then turned to us.

His remark staggered us. 'Well, that's OK. I thought you didn't want me to see your child. I thought she might have been coloured!' Australia at that time operated a White Only policy; any trace of coloured blood and we would have been turned down as undesirable. The All White policy has since been moderated. Mr Foster was not in the least interested in anyone who wanted to go to Queensland as he said, 'I'm a Victoria man myself.' (We learned that the rivalry between the states is even more pronounced than that which exists between Lancashire and Yorkshire!)

His visit lasted about an hour and we breathed a sigh of relief when he had gone. All we had to do now was to wait for the letter of acceptance. Our families weren't very happy at the thought of our going so far away, but realised that it might be the best thing to do; at least we knew it would only be for two years if it turned out to be a mistake.

Early in the new year we had our letter of acceptance, also details of the date when our baggage would be collected, leaving only our hand luggage to be taken on the day of embarkation. We began to dispose of our furniture – our china, glass and bedding we would take with us. It was quite sad to see our home disappearing by degrees: our handmade rugs, small items of furniture which Ron had made, our Utility dining room suite which we had taken such pride in, mahogany and highly polished. The flat became as bare as Mother Hubbard's cupboard; soon we were left with only a few necessities, and when were were notified of our sailing date, we had only nine days to complete our arrangements.

We spent the last few days at my parents' home, saying our 'Goodbyes' to friends and relatives. The name of the ship we were to journey on was the SS *Orsova*, the flagship of the Orient Fleet, a 32,000 ton vessel on her maiden voyage. The March morning of our departure was bitterly cold, a north-east wind blowing, not a good day to start a sea journey. My parents came to the station to see us off. No one likes goodbyes and ours was brief. Promises to write often, to take care of ourselves, our luggage put into the guard's van, the whistle blowing and we were off. As the train went straight into a tunnel there was no time to wave and Vivienne was promptly sick, all over herself and us. The smell was appalling and in the turmoil of trying to clean ourselves up, we had no time for tears. It wasn't a very auspicious start to a five-week journey but as the train neared London, I began to feel more cheerful. After all, wasn't this to be the trip of a lifetime?

Chapter 2

The Journey

My expectations of our voyage were quickly shattered. The train journey to Tilbury was dismal, everything bleak and grey. The flat featureless landscape stretched each side of the railway tracks, such trees as there were bent low by the bitter wind. I began then, I think, to realise what a pleasant part of the country I had always lived in. On our arrival at the port itself all was bustle and confusion, crowds of people everywhere, voices echoing through the high buildings, porters' trolleys laden with luggage; it seemed utter chaos. We passed through Passport Control, weighing in our baggage, and on to a small walkway. In front of us were rows of windows, the walls surrounding them painted a pale biscuit colour.

'Well, there she is,' said my husband.

'Who?'

'The ship of course, the *Orsova*.'

I stared at the numerous windows. 'I thought it was another building.' I was no stranger to ships (I had been on many of them as a visitor, during my father's naval career) but not like this! I looked upward and the windows seemed to go on for ever, until I could see an upper deck, and then the funnel, topped by an enormous Welsh hat type of pot. If I had seen the liner afloat on the ocean it would have been recognisable, but to encounter it through a door, it could have been any large building.

Once aboard we were directed to our cabins, on a lower deck, well below the water mark. The cabins were very small, containing only the bare necessities. Men and women were segregated and I was to share with a Mrs Greaves and her three children and, of course, my own daughter. There

5

were three two-tiered bunks, a wash-hand basin, a six–drawered chest which stood underneath the porthole (no windows on this deck!) and an alcove curtained off to hang dresses and coats in. For over a month we were going to be cooped up in this tiny space, to sleep, wash, dress and keep all our personal belongings. Six of us. It was going to be a tight fit! The thought was daunting.

We unpacked and went up to the dining saloon to find Ron. We sailed at two p.m. on that bitter afternoon. There were a few wellwishers and relatives waving from the quayside, the band played 'Now is the hour' and 'Life on the Ocean Wave', tears and waves, scarves and handerchiefs fluttered and the great ship moved slowly into the estuary. Lifeboat drill was called for three p.m. We had all been informed of our correct stations in case of emergency and were wearing our life jackets.

With over two and a half thousand people on board, including the crew, it was quite a performance to assemble everyone in their correct positions. As we stood in our groups, the deck began to tilt at an alarming angle.

'Whatever is happening?' I gasped.

Ron looked at me strangely. 'Nothing is happening – what do you mean?'

'Look at the deck, the rails, everything is tilting.'

'Are you all right? You look odd. Nothing is tilting. I think it is you.'

I said, 'I don't feel too good. As soon as this drill is over I'll go and lie down in my cabin.'

That was to be the pattern of the next few weeks. I certainly spent a great deal of the voyage in a horizontal position! I hadn't realised that sea sickness could give rise to so many strange symptoms. The food on board was superb, the menu varied day after day, such delicious dishes as we had never seen. Food was still on the ration in England, and items that weren't actually on ration were in very short supply, so to most passengers mealtimes were a source of delight. I can't say how delightful as *my* diet consisted mainly of dry bread rolls and a little fruit!

For me the voyage was a disaster: whenever the ship was actually moving, I felt ill. In spite of some tablets called Kwells, which turned my skin a sickly yellow, nothing helped the nausea. Sometimes in the dining room I would see something on the menu that I thought I could eat, so I would order it. As soon as the steward brought it and set the plate in front of me I would snatch up a bread roll and beat a hasty retreat! Ron feels I should qualify for a place in the Guinness Book of Records as the only person to be sick while travelling down the Suez Canal!

The only time I felt really well was when swimming in the pool. I am sure that if my meals could have been served to me on a floating tray during a swim, I could have eaten and enjoyed them.

Surprisingly, I found life in the cabin easier than I had expected. The children were well behaved and Mrs Greaves very pleasant. Her husband had been in Australia for about a year and had finally found a home for them. The boy, who was ten, was particularly looking forward to seeing his father. The two girls were much younger and had forgotten much about him. I was soon to find that Mrs Greaves was more than pleasant – she shared her affections not only with her children, but with several of the crew as well! Invariably the children were put to bed early while mother went off to entertain and be entertained in the crew's quarters. Vivienne, being only three years old, was always in bed early, so I became night nanny to them all. Mrs Greaves would arrive back in the cabin, to occupy her bunk for about an hour, before the steward brought the morning tea.

Ron shared a cabin with a lad of twenty, going out to live with his sister in Queensland. He came from a small village in Gloucestershire, and was very immature, totally unprepared to face the big wide world. We could not imagine how he had made the decision to leave his parents and village to travel so far. We nicknamed him 'The Shadow' as he followed us everywhere; if we turned around, Donald was there.

The other occupants of Ron's cabin were Fred, a Londoner in his fifties, and his six-year-old son, Billy. Fred's wife Kate, and Grace, their teenage daughter, were sharing a cabin with four other women in the next corridor. Fred had been a hairdresser in London and was going out to join grown-up sons. He was a born comic and a great brass band enthusiast. He would sit for ages, lost in a dream world, where he played, in mime, every instrument from a trumpet to a tuba, making all the appropriate noises. Totally oblivious to the stares of fellow passengers, he would keep us all highly entertained. So these few people, with whom we lived in such close proximity, became like old friends during the long voyage.

In spite of my continual sickness, I did enjoy all the trips ashore. I had never been abroad before and my first sight of 'Foreign Parts' was an unforgettable experience. Strictly speaking, it wasn't foreign at all. After several days at sea, including a rough crossing of the Bay of Biscay, we reached Gibraltar. It was early morning and the famous Rock was just peeping above the mist. As we drew into port the swirls of mist began to lift and the rays of the sun tipped the peaks. A bugler from the regiment stationed there began to play Reveille, the Union Jack was unfurled and the sun caught the brass bugle and the lines of soldiers and turned them to gold. I felt the whole incident had been arranged specially for me! It was so impressive that I have never forgotten it.

All the places we visited were so different from each other; now that most people travel by air, such a variety of experiences are missed. Once aboard an aircraft, there is nothing to see, at least only from a great height. The Bay of Naples must surely be one of the loveliest natural harbours. The palm trees along the waterfront with the volcano in the background, turned purple and blue when the sun went down. The narrow streets with their tall houses, washing stretched across every balcony, dark doorways where women sat, their numerous children darting in and out, brown and barefooted. Scrawny hens, tied by one leg, pecked about in the dust. I feel we saw much more of the 'real' Naples, down there near the dockside, than the passengers who went on a guided tour with a courier.

We did venture further into the town, to visit some of the beautiful old churches, and had tea and cakes in a palatial restaurant. The decor did not extend to the toilet, which was in the basement, approached through a cellar occupied by a crowd of card-playing Italians. I passed them, feeling rather embarrassed, to find the so-called toilet was only a hole in the wall! The silver tea service we had used, and the bone china, were a far cry from the other facilities.

The Mediterranean Sea was a great disappointment. There was such a thick fog we could see nothing. I was lying on my bunk, feeling as if I didn't care if the ship went to the bottom, when the door burst open and two crew members rushed in. They apologised hurriedly and explained that as the weather was growing worse, all portholes must be covered. They were certainly right about the weather! It was appalling. Although a new ship with the latest kind of stabilisers, the motion was dreadful. According to Ron, the dining room was half empty and few people had any appetite for the next twelve hours. I did not leave the cabin until I felt I could walk without falling over. Ron had been amused to see a steward carrying a plate with a set of dentures on it, asking if anyone knew the owner!

Port Said was our next port of call. We were allowed to go ashore for the day on condition that we signed a document to say we did so at our own risk, the political situation being unstable at that time. It never occurred to us that we might be in any real danger and we thoroughly enjoyed our visit, accompanied by our 'Shadow' Donald. We hired an open carriage to see the sights and spent some time in the local bazaars, where we bargained for a large leather pouffe. Judging by the number of passengers that returned clutching similar ones, I think the local traders must have had a field day.

From Port Said, we sailed down the Suez Canal and through the Bitter Lakes. The ship moved very slowly down the Canal as the wash damaged the banks if any excessive speed was maintained. At intervals huge dredgers were moored, ready to deal with any problems of bank repair. The road that runs parallel was quite busy with traffic. Enormous cars, Cadillacs and Studebakers purred by, no doubt driven by oil-rich Arabs. Camels trailed across the desert in long caravans and their riders waved to us, but in spite of the apparent friendliness, men crouched in the rushes lining the Canal, their guns trained on the ship. We did not understand the political situation at all but began to feel like sitting ducks as we sat by the rails. The sunset over the desert was magnificent, brilliant red turning to orange, lemon and then deep purple as the sudden darkness fell. Camels hunched in the sand, their shapes vaguely outlined by the lights from the ship, a pin-prick of red betraying the position of their masters as they lit their cigarettes, and in the still air, the pungent odours of tobacco and camel dung mingled. We really felt we were in the heart of the mysterious East.

The heat as we journeyed on towards Aden grew unbearable and many of the passengers had to be treated in the sick bay for 'heat exhaustion'; we were lucky to remain free. Aden, which was then a duty free port, was interesting. Narrow streets teemed with people; camels and goats roamed freely; the noise was harsh to our ears and dust stung our eyes. An orchestra was playing on a balcony over a carpet shop, loud and discordant to us but no doubt tuneful to the local population. Women glided by, shrouded and veiled, heads low, as became their status; small boys pestered us to buy trashy jewellery or cheap watches and shopkeepers pleaded with us to enter their open-fronted shops and view their wares. The goods were so cheap and we were tempted but our budget was very limited so we resisted. We did buy a small wooden chalet which, when opened, played 'Auld Lang Syne' – not a very Eastern souvenir!

As it grew dark the town became even more alive. Arabs with stalls selling exotic foods cried out their prices and the spicy smells hung in the hot air. Barrows piled high with sickly-looking sweetmeats attracted the small boys, with their trays of watches and necklaces hung around their necks. Ron weakened and bought a wristwatch from one pathetic-looking waif. It actually turned out to be a very good timekeeper, far superior to the one he had brought from home.

String *charpoys* were set up beside the roads as the evening wore on, and skinny men lay down to sleep. Others, with their camels, lay in the gutters, curled beside the great beasts, their heads resting against the smelly creatures, everyone unconcerned with the passers-by. With little or no rainfall in Aden, there was no fear of a soaking in the night.

The shops showed no sign of closing: all the while there were ships in port there were customers to be had, and they were ready. It was about three in the morning when we returned to the ship and stood at the rails watching Aden recede, the distant lights of the shops twinkling through the darkness and the noise fading as we steamed slowly out to sea.

Between Aden and Ceylon, now known as Sri Lanka, the sea was very rough. This was usual, so we were told, but unpleasant nevertheless. I remarked to a fellow passenger that in spite of the weather, I felt quite safe. 'After all, this is a new ship with every safety device possible,' I said. 'So was the Titanic!' was the short reply. Not much comfort!

Being in a cabin below the water mark was like being in a washing machine, I thought. The porthole didn't open, but as the ship rolled, sometimes the sky was visible, other times just the deep water. I half expected to see a fish gliding by.

It was so humid by now that many of the passengers were sleeping on deck. We had only pillows and blankets from our cabins and the boards were hard, but it was better than the stuffy atmosphere below decks. We spent the rest of the voyage sleeping under the stars. I'm afraid I abandoned the Greaves children, letting their mother know that I would not be with them. One disadvantage of sleeping on deck was the early morning cry of 'Show a leg,' when there would be an undignified scramble as we gathered up pillows and blankets and fled before the onslaught of the hoses as the decks were sluiced down.

The *Orsova* was in a somewhat unfinished state. During the sea trials at Barrow-in-Furness, a steam pressure gauge had been left open one night, and had not been noticed by the night watch. The result had been that the adhesive had melted behind the laminated plastic sheeting which lined with walls, so all the floors in the entire ship were spotted with glutinous patches, dark and still sticky. It had been feared that the ship would not have been able to sail on time, as a number of repairs had to be made. The sailing date had been adhered to but there were many finishing touches to be done.

At Naples several dozen young Italian men had been recruited to clean the ship. They literally scrubbed their way to Australia. In every corridor and lounge they were to be seen, scraping glue from the floors or cleaning paintwork.

One day all passengers received a letter from the Purser's Office, stating that a refund of ten percent would be made to everybody because of the inconvenience suffered. Ron and I queried this as we, like many others on board, were assisted passengers and had only paid ten pounds each. We were told that we were perfectly entitled to the refund on the full fare, so we actually got back more than we had paid! A free voyage and some more spending money into the bargain!

Our fellow passengers were from all races; some were tourists just enjoying a cruise, others were Australians returning home after a visit to the 'Old Country' as they called it; many, like ourselves, starting a new life. There were several Sikhs going home to India, some Orthodox Jews always wearing their black hats and their hair in little ringlets and a group of Egyptians going out on a business visit. It was the differing behaviour of these fellow passengers that made them stand out from the others.

The Sikhs were fine-looking men, tall, with their dark eyes and huge turbans, black beards and reserved manner. Each evening at sundown they would kneel on the deck and chant their prayers, a sad haunting sound. The Jews, who were all very young men, would walk the decks continually, reading aloud from their open books, in a language I assumed to be Hebrew. The Egyptians talked together with much loud laughter and gesticulations, always seeming excited. One man whose appearance we awaited each evening was a Scot. As the sun set, he would appear in full Highland dress, complete with his bagpipes, and march up and down, playing such mournful tunes, long after dark. We would groan, 'There he goes again, "Over the Sea to Skye".' We wished fervently that he would!

There was a short obese man with an enormous belly. Red raw from sunburn, he wore the briefest of shorts, and seemed quite proud of his grotesque shape. He was nicknamed 'Mr Five by Five' – very appropriate! At one of the fancy dress balls he appeared draped in a white sheet, an Egyptian fez and a pair of dark glasses. As King Farouk, he was easily recognisable; he certainly did not need the padding!

Every evening there were film shows, tombola, greyhound racing with wooden dogs drawn by wire, dances and talent shows, all of which helped to pass the time. Contrary to popular belief, a long voyage can be really boring – nothing to do but eat, drink and enjoy yourself! There were Landfall Dinners whenever we were due to visit another port. These were usually buffets with the most elaborate concoctions. The long tables had wonderful centre–pieces; enormous horns of pastry spilling out all kinds of confections; whole salmon with unusual dressings; baskets of marzipan, laden with sugar and fruits; such gastronomic sights almost impossible to describe. Whilst I could gaze in wonder, my appetite remained the same – bread rolls and a small amount of fruit!

The people we mixed with mostly were the families who shared our corridors or dining tables, and of course, Donald, Fred and family. One day as we sat on deck, Fred came up to us in a state of great agitation. He leaned close to Ron and said in a hoarse whisper, 'What are we going to do?'

Ron answered, puzzled, 'Do? About what?'

'Well, you know, this shared cabin business. I mean, well – you know, we have been at sea nearly three weeks and – well – I LOVE MY WIFE!' His voice had risen almost to a shout, his expression so anguished that we had to smother a desire to laugh. He went on, 'We never get five minutes alone; even if the kids are otherwise occupied, there is always Donald! If I turn around, there he is.'

Ron chuckled, 'I can see your problem, Fred, but I don't see what I can do about it, unless one day when Billy and Grace are at a film or something, you can give me a nod and I'll see that Donald stays with us, and let you and Kate have an hour together.'

Fred was delighted, 'Thanks mate, then I'll do the same for you!'

Ron pulled a face, pointing at my reclining figure. 'I don't think there will be much likelihood of that. Take a look at my other half. When she isn't being sick, she's asleep!'

The afternoon came when there was a special children's entertainment arranged. I was in my usual horizontal position in a deck chair and Ron was playing deck quoits with Donald. Fred appeared at the doorway to the games deck and gave Ron a thumbs-up sign. Ron returned it with a grin and Fred disappeared down the staircase leading to our corridors. At the end of one game, Donald went through to the bar to get himself a lemonade. When he hadn't returned after ten minutes, Ron went to look for him. He came back. 'I hope to goodness he hasn't gone down to the cabin for anything. Fred will never let me forget it if he has.'

'Why should he have gone down?' We searched the deck with no success. Some minutes later, Donald returned, red-faced and flustered. 'I say, don't you think this is an awful cheek? I went down to our cabin – there is a ship coming this way and I wanted my camera. The door was locked on the inside. I knocked and knocked and no one answered. I waited ages and called out, then at last the door opened just a crack and it was Fred! He said I couldn't come in as Kate was in there, having a wash down. Why can't she use her own cabin? And anyway, there are plenty of showers and baths at the end of the corridor. What do you think of that?'

Ron took Donald to one side, and while not exactly telling him about the birds and the bees, he explained, as simply as possible, that couples do like to be alone sometimes. Donald's face was a picture. He grew even redder and his mouth formed a huge 'OH.' 'Why didn't he say so then?' He was rather confused but agreed that if another time we asked him to stay with us, he would not return to the cabin.

Fred's remarks when he finally came up on deck were not repeatable! The experiment was not a success and wasn't tried again.

We sailed into the port of Colombo early one beautiful morning. A cool breeze was blowing and the Island of Ceylon looked lush and green. There were white sandy shores lapped by the bluest of seas, fringed by palm trees, bright tropical flowers tumbled everywhere, and the sound of surf rang in our ears. In the streets bullock carts rumbled along, looking like the old covered wagons of the American West. Bicycles spun past and a multitude of people hurried about their daily business, spotless in their white robes. Lovely girls in saris of every colour glided gracefully along, the small red marks in the centre of their foreheads proclaiming their caste.

We went eagerly ashore. We had booked a tour of the island by coach and were fascinated by the sights, sounds and smells around us. The visit to a Buddhist temple, where we left our shoes outside, was quite an experience. Statues of gods and goddesses, studded with jewels, brooded over the incense-heavy silence. We were not allowed to take any pictures and it is difficult to describe the atmosphere, but the wealth around us, the marble altars, the gold ornaments, the winking rubies and emeralds, contrasted starkly with the poverty of the district we had recently driven through. We had stopped in a small mountain village where the residents were washing themselves and their linen in a communal fountain. Women with leprous faces and bodies begged us for money, several of them holding tiny babies to their withered, sagging breasts. I was horrified and couldn't believe that these old, sick-looking women actually were the mothers of these babies.

One of them came close to us, feeding her scrawny child, and thrust her face into mine. Her nose had been completely eaten away and one ear had almost gone. She whined and held out a skinny arm. I turned away, almost sick, but Ron placed some coins into her outstretched palm and she turned and crept into the trees. I looked at our daughter, rosy-cheeked and sturdy, and wondered then, as I have many times since, what sort of world we live in that can hold such contrasts.

As the day wore on it grew even hotter and all the ladies on the coach bought pretty painted fans from a street stall, with which we created a little air in the stifling coach. It had no air-conditioning and was almost unbearable.

We came to an area where there were fishmarkets and our Ceylonese guide said, 'Ladies and Gentleman, we are now approaching the fishmarket.' Fred's raucous Cockney voice came from the back seat, 'Blimey mate, I'm glad you told us, we'd never have known.' There was general laughter; the smell was so appalling that it remained in the coach long after the markets had been left behind.

By mid-afternoon we were in a district called Mount Lavinia. We stopped at a gracious hotel. Shades of the Raj! The rooms were high and vaulted with tiled floors and *punkahs* swishing gently to and fro, the cords pulled by small, brown-eyed dark-skinned boys. It was a relief to be able to wash in cool lemon-scented water and sit in comfortable cane chairs on a spacious verandah.

Servants padded silently around, serving us with tea in fine china cups, and plates of delicious cakes and scones. We were high on a hillside; the forest stretched in terraces below, to the shimmering sea. As we sat sipping our tea, a long line of elephants emerged from the trees, their *mahouts* riding high on their backs, and trailed across the white sand towards the water. The riders slipped to the ground and the great beasts rolled and wallowed in the surf, sending spurts of water through their trunks up into the air. They bellowed and trumpeted their pleasure as the water surged around them.

The azure sky, the green of the tropical vegetation and the sparkling, dancing waves, with these gentle, giant creatures bathing the dust from their bodies is a sight I shall never forget.

We sailed that evening, in the best romantic tradition, into the sunset, leaving behind an island bathed in the after-glow of the brilliant colours of the sinking sun, surely everyone's picture of Paradise. Now that Ceylon has been renamed Sri Lanka and is beset by political problems, I have often wondered if the ordinary inhabitants' lifestyle has changed.

The largest stretch now faced us, the Indian Ocean. It would be eight days before we sighted land again, at Fremantle. The weather was extremely hot, although with the ship moving at a fair speed, there was usually a little breeze. We were nearing the Equator where the ceremony of 'Crossing the Line' would take place. I don't know the origins of this rite, but I remember my Father telling me about it: he had 'crossed the line' a number of times in his Naval days. Not everyone would participate but all the volunteers who had been selected lined up one afternoon, by the swimming pool. Burly sailors, in all kinds of strange dress, processed along the deck – King Neptune in a skirt of seaweed, a long beard and complete with trident; Queen Titania in blonde wig and more seaweed with a brassiere made from coconut shells, barbers and surgeons following behind. Crowds of passengers jostled for a good view and there was much laughter as the unwary volunteers were pounced upon.

They were 'shaved' by barbers, who smothered them with masses of sticky foam and wielded gigantic 'razors', operated on by yelling 'surgeons' who supposedly slit open their stomachs, producing long strings of sausages and all kinds of revolting offal. They were embraced by the husky Queen Titania and finally flung into the pool to be seized upon by Neptune himself. He gave them a thorough ducking before they were rescued by the motley crowd of helpers. I was glad I had not volunteered but it was all great fun for the watchers! Every passenger was given a certificate to say we had 'Crossed the Line' and must in future be given the freedom of the Seven Seas and were under the protection of King Neptune and his court for ever!

That night there was a gala dinner with fancy dress and again, a selection of dishes to make the mouth water. We actually crossed the Equator during the night and it was very cold. We were sleeping on deck and had to scurry for shelter as it poured with rain. During the days we enjoyed watching the dolphins that followed the ship, playing together, such graceful creatures; sharks too, their fins protruding above the water. Countless flying fish, a flash of silver as they skimmed over the surface, and the dark blue jellyfish, their long tentacles floating beneath them.

It wasn't all fun and games though. Halfway across the Ocean, one of the passengers, a lady in her sixties, travelling alone to visit her daughter in Sydney, died. Apparently, the heat had been too much for her and she suffered a heart attack. A notice from the purser was circulated, asking if we would go to the funeral service on the upper deck at sunset of that same day. The engines would be stopped for about half an hour. It was eerie, the enormous ship, wallowing silently in an empty sea, the sun sinking, and the body, draped in a Union Jack, resting on a trestle. I thought how sad it was, to die alone, so far from home, and even sadder for the family awaiting her arrival.

The service was brief, conducted by the ship's chaplain, and the band played 'Eternal Father' as the corpse was slipped over the side. I remarked to our steward that night what an unfortunate thing to happen and his reply surprised me.

'Have you thought, if you live in a village of over two thousand people, that in a period of over a month it would not be unusual if someone died. This ship is really just like a floating village isn't it?' I suppose that was quite true.

The night before we docked at Fremantle there was a final Landfall

Dinner – competitions, fancy dress and lovely prizes. One passenger won a basket of all kinds of fruit, bedecked with ribbons, a real work of art. Next morning we stood at the rails to say our farewells to those of our fellow passengers who were disembarking. The lady who had won the fruit basket approached the gangway. She was stopped by two customs officers.

'Just a minute, madam. You can't take that fruit ashore. No plants or fruit allowed.'

'But I won it last night,' she protested.

'Sorry, you'll have to leave it with us.'

'That I won't.' She was indignant. 'Surely I could keep the basket?'

'If you like.' The customs officer was curt. She took out the apples and oranges and rolled them along the deck towards the onlookers, thrust pineapples, grapes, bananas, paw-paws and passion fruit into the arms of people at the rails and with her suitcase in one hand and the empty basket in the other, she marched down the gangplank in high dudgeon! I thought it was such a pity the prize hadn't been won by someone who was continuing the journey.

We said goodbye and wished good luck to many of our companions, some, like Jack and Janey, with their daughter Rene, whom we would meet again. Also to Frank and Jean, with their three children, James, Janet and Lillian, who were much later to become good friends of ours.

After all the formalities had been completed for the passengers leaving, the rest of us were allowed ashore. Many of us went by coach into Perth, a pleasant city situated on the Swan River, with its famous black swans. Perth had some fine shops and parks and we were quite impressed with the city.

Adelaide was our next port of call, across the Great Australian Bight. We had dreaded this part of the journey. The Bight had a reputation of very rough seas. In the event, it was like a millpond, not a ripple in sight!

Adelaide is known as the city of churches with an old world charm about it. We spent a day there, somewhat spoiled by the bush fires raging on the outskirts so that a pall of smoke hung over everything.

At Melbourne, the dock workers were on strike and we were moored there for three days. We were ashore most of the time, exploring the city and surrounding districts, returning to the ship to sleep. By this time, my seasickness had become a permanent feature of my life, so that, although stationary, the nausea was just as bad. Nothing like nausea to put a damper on an outing!

Mrs Greaves left the ship here and I was amused to see her fall into her husband's arms for a blissful reunion! They kissed passionately and I did wonder if her conscience pricked a little!

Forty-eight hours later we packed our belongings to be stacked on deck ready for unloading the next day, retaining only our hand luggage. At sunrise the following morning we lined the decks as the ship steamed slowly up the Sydney Heads and under the famous Coathanger Bridge. It was a stirring sight, flotillas of small craft accompanying us, jets of water spraying high in the air, their whistles and hooters sounding. The maiden voyage was over and our new life about to begin.

Chapter 3

The New Beginning

We disembarked as soon as we had eaten our breakfasts, and stood on the quayside watching the huge nets lowering our trunks and boxes. The passengers who were staying in the area were dealt with first; quite a number of them were going to a camp some miles from the city. Those of us going on to Queensland were left until later. Our train was not due to leave until the evening so there was plenty of time. We recognised our baggage and saw it trundled into the customs shed. Fred and Kate were standing with us and suddenly Kate said, 'There's our big packing case, Fred. Oh, I do hope they are careful with it.' She turned to me. 'I marked it FRAGILE. It has all our china and glass in it.'

As we watched, the net containing her precious belongings swung perilously to and fro. Kate was almost dancing up and down with agitation. She called out to the crane operator, 'Please, please be careful with that one, it's my best china.'

The man looked down at us, made a two–fingered gesture and released some mechanism, causing the net to crash to the ground. We stood, staring, unbelieving, Kate almost in tears.

'Rotten sod,' she choked. 'I'm sure that was no accident. All our wedding presents, Fred, things we have taken such care of all these years, they must be in pieces.'

Fred was seething. He put his arms around her shoulders and said, 'Don't make a fuss, please. He will only drop the rest of our things.' We all moved away, hardly able to take in what had happened.

Fred and Ron went to the customs shed to supervise the clearance of our effects and to arrange for them to be put on the same train with us in the evening. Kate and her children were meeting some old neighbours in the waiting room and spending the day with them, while Vivienne and I were expecting to be met by a girl I had worked with some years before. We arranged to meet our husbands at the railway station in the later afternoon and went to the exit.

Daisy and I had only exchanged Christmas cards since she left home some two years previously, but when I knew the date of our arrival, I had let her know. She was waiting for us, with her husband, Cyril. They had travelled in on the coach that was to take some of our fellow passengers to the camp where they lived with their two young sons. We boarded the coach and, when the luggage had been loaded, we set off. I was quite eager to see all the sights as we drove through the city, the view of the famous bridge from the shoreside, all the modern buildings among the old shops and so on. We began to leave the centre behind and as we stopped at some traffic lights I noticed a group of people making signs at us, clenched fists and facial grimaces. A little further on it happened again and this time I heard what they said.

'Another load of Pommie bastards!'

I turned to Daisy. 'What do they mean? Don't they like us?'

She shook her head, 'Take no notice; it is always like that. They know this is the hostel bus. You soon get used to it.'

I was shocked. All the leaflets and information we had read before we left home had painted such a rosy picture. Nothing had prepared me for this. If the people of Australia didn't want us, why were we so encouraged to come? The hostel was another surprise. It was just an untidy sprawl of old Nissen huts. Daisy and Cyril had a large one, partitioned across the centre, their children sleeping in one half, themselves in the other. Their food was eaten in a communal dining room; toilets and showers were in blocks set apart from the huts. In fact, it looked like the Army barracks it probably once was.

They did have a small stove on which they could make a snack or a bedtime drink. I was curious and asked Daisy, 'Tell me honestly, are you really happy here?'

She replied, 'I absolutely hate it. We wish we had never come, but it's too late now. If we ever did get the chance to go home, what would we do? Cyril is so much older than me and he has no real trade. It would be so hard for him to get a job. We must make the best of it now.' She looked so dejected, I felt how lucky we were to be going to a flat and not a Nissen hut! They came back to the dock area with us about five o'clock and I felt quite depressed as I waved them goodbye. Ron was still in the customs shed, after all those hours, and I wondered what could be wrong. He finally caught up with us as we stood with Fred, Kate and family, waiting to board the train.

'Whatever happened to you? I was afraid you would miss the train.'

'You wouldn't believe it, all this time in the customs shed and *now* they won't release our main baggage.'

I was annoyed. 'Why? We have only got the usual things. What's the problem?'

'Don't ask me! I have had the most frustrating day, ending with a real row.'

It appeared that our hand baggage had been put on the train but our big trunk and boxes had been put aside, along with some of the other passengers' effects. There was a dispute among the workers, just as there had been in Melbourne. Added to this, there was evidently a lot of anti-British feeling. When Ron had insisted on being told the reason for the impounding of our effects, the reply had been, 'You bloody Poms, coming out here, trying to take over our jobs, wanting everything your own way.'

Ron had been stung into replying, 'Well, as far as I can see, I would probably make a better fist of it than you do!'

That hadn't helped and so here we were, boarding the train with only the few clothes we were wearing and our overnight bags with our toilet requirements, but no bedding, saucepans or china or any of the basic needs to set up in our new home. Ron had eaten nothing since breakfast on the ship, early in the morning, so he wasn't very cheerful. The train stopped at intervals during the night and hot coffee, rolls and crisps were available from the trolleys on the platform. We had no sleeping berths and were somewhat crowded in our carriage so it wasn't a comfortable journey. With daylight, my spirits rose. I love train journeys – it is the only form of transport that doesn't make me feel sick!

There had been heavy rainfalls in New South Wales and Queensland and many of the bridges had been washed away. The train was diverted several times, held back in sidings, then continuing on a different route, and everywhere we could see the devastation caused by the floods. Where the water had rushed through, trees had been uprooted and small animals were perched on the branches, no doubt bewildered at finding their natural homes at ground level. Flocks of small coloured birds, probably budgerigars, swept to and fro, their chattering audible even to us in the moving train. Gradually we left the floods behind and the greenery began to give way to unfamiliar trees of a greyish colour.

Kangaroo were a common sight, often standing watching the train, chewing leaves and branches. They were huge beasts, well over five feet tall, but so gentle-looking. The termite hills fascinated me, enormous heaps of earth, close together, giving an almost prehistoric look to the landscape.

About mid-day we had a lunch stop. Right beside the enormous engine a trestle table had been laid along the platform. All the 'Assisted Passage' travellers were seated here to await a meal. And await it we did! As the minutes ticked away and no food was forthcoming, we grew impatient. We were all hungry and we had been told it would only be a short stop. Eventually two young girls appeared and started to place plates of food in front of us. It looked like steak and kidney pie, with potatoes and pumpkin, which was a new vegetable to us. The meat was so tough no one could manage it. All along the table jaws were moving up and down, but it was impossible to swallow it! Gradually the rim of each plate was decorated with lumps of revolting gristle. A voice from the far end of the table piped up.

'Steak and kidney, she told us! Well, it's a long time since I tasted such meat, but I bet that piece never saw a cow! Kangaroo more likely!'

We all laughed. We had been told how tough kangaroo meat was so he could well have been right. Before we had half finished our meal the engine gave a shrill whistle and let off a hiss of steam so fierce that several of the children screamed in fright. Then a cloud of smuts descended on us, all over the table and the contents of our plates. I felt it was an apt comment. Once again the whistle, the steam and the smuts, then the guard shouting,

'Hurry up youse all, train's leaving.'

The table was abandoned, just as the two girls appeared, wheeling a trolley, presumably bearing our pudding. We scrambled aboard, hardly having time to shut the doors before we were in motion, dirty, tired and still hungry.

The landscape was changing, becoming more tropical-looking, with exotic trees and flowers. There was no water left on the train by this time and we all wished the journey was over. It was late evening by the time we drew into Brisbane Central Station. We said 'Goodbye' to our companions – it was almost like leaving our families again. After so many weeks together it was quite sad. We exchanged addresses with Fred and Kate, wished each other luck and parted. The couple who had been our sponsors were not able to meet us and a neighbour had agreed to come instead. She was a middle-aged lady and had a couple of teenagers with her. We assumed they were her own offspring. I was longing to finish the journey. The thought of a long cold drink and a hot bath was a tempting prospect. We had understood from the letters we had exchanged that our flat was close to the city. In fact it was almost thirty miles distant.

We had very little money left and our escort soon let us know she had none! There was one train which would take us part of the way but the last eight miles would have to be undertaken by taxi, if we could find one! The local train was comprised of two small coaches, like mini-buses joined together. At the tiny halt where it terminated we alighted with our few pieces of luggage and set about trying to find a taxi. We asked the few passers-by if they knew of one, and finally found an address to go to. The cab owner was out but if we cared to wait, we could. As it was the only taxi available we didn't have much choice, and settled down on a seat under a tree. I felt as if I had been travelling for ever. The night was hot and the scent of the tropical flowers around us and the continual hum and buzz of the myriad strange insects had an almost hypnotic effect on me. We weren't talking. Vivienne was asleep in Ron's arms and the time dragged on. When the battered old taxi finally arrived we were all dozing. The owner obviously didn't want another job at that time of night but we explained our predicament, agreed on a price, and squeezed ourselves into the vehicle. He stopped on a dirt road, dark and dusty and held out his hand. 'That'll cost you eight pounds, sport, it's further than I thought,' he said, and waited. That left us with about five pounds but Ron paid him without comment. Our companion pointed to a house with a light in the upper floor, said 'Mind the cattle grid, see you around,' and with her girls disappeared into the darkness.

We picked our way across the iron grid, through long grass, sending up a swarm of noisy insects, and arrived at the house. Like most in that part of Queensland, it stood on high stilts, a long flight of wooden stairs leading up to the door. A man stood in the doorway, tall and white-haired.

'Welcome to Queensland,' he said in a broad Australian accent.

We climbed wearily up the stairs, Vivienne still deeply asleep in Ron's arms, while I carried the baggage. The door opened into a room, long and narrow, and unbelievably filthy. A bench ran along one side, under the window, littered with spare parts of bicycles, oily rags, opened tins of baked beans, soup, condensed milk, and other half-eaten oddments. On the other side of the room stood a camp bed with a jumble of bedclothes on it. A chair and a small cupboard were the only other pieces of furniture. It wasn't this which riveted my attention though, but the insects! The walls were crawling with such a variety of livestock, huge brown cockroaches, moths and flying insects, the like of which I had never seen. I was appalled. The man, who apparently was the owner of the house, was saying something, and I dragged my attention back to him.

'I expect you are tired, you're very late. Your flat is through there.' He pointed to a stained sheet covering the doorway.

'Go in and make yourselves at home. I'll tell Jean you've arrived. She's been saving you a meal.'

He disappeared out of the door and down the stairs. Jean, our sponsor, and her family evidently lived somewhere below.

We went though into our 'flat': a small bedroom which contained two beds with mosquito nets, a chair, and a curtained alcove which led into the other room. The living room had a sink, an ancient electric cooker, a small table and two chairs and a wall cupboard. A lobby led to a toilet and basin, shared, we supposed, with our landlord. Ron laid Vivienne on the smaller bed and we stood looking at each other. He spoke first.

'What on earth have I brought you to?'

I tried to sound cheerful. 'It's probably not as bad as it looks. We shall feel quite different when we have had a meal, a wash and a good sleep. Tomorrow we can clean the place up a bit.'

Ron didn't seem convinced. 'Let's hope that Jean got some stores with the money you sent from Fremantle.'

We looked in the kitchen cupboard. There was a half pound of margarine, a loaf, a packet of tea and a pint of milk.

'Not much, I'm afraid, but she is bringing up a meal and we can shop in Brisbane tomorrow after we have been to the bank and drawn some money.'

We heard heavy footsteps coming up the outer stairs and Jean appeared in the doorway. She was carrying a tray with two plates on it. Food at last! We introduced ourselves and sat thankfully down to eat. She stood watching us, a large raw–boned woman with huge arms and legs. She wore a blouse and a short skirt and was barefooted. She evidently suffered a skin problem as her limbs were covered with enormous sores. She had cooked us sausages, potatoes and green beans. I was about to tuck in when I saw, right in the middle of the beans, a knot of black hair, as if the debris from a comb had dropped into the cooking pot. Fork halfway to my mouth I stopped. 'What's the matter?' she asked. Ron looked at me curiously.

'I don't feel very hungry. I think I am just too tired to eat.'

It sounded very lame and I think Jean was offended, but I couldn't swallow a morsel. Ron was eating and I dared not look at his plate.

'We would like to go to Brisbane in the morning; what time do the buses go?' I was determined to change the subject.

'Buses? You mean the bus. There's only one each day. It comes somewhere around six thirty. You have to be outside soon after six, in case he comes early. He goes a long way round so you don't get to Brisbane until nearly nine. He leaves again at four, so don't miss it or you'll have to hitch a lift.'

'Doesn't that make it difficult to get a job, then?' Ron asked.

'Oh, you can't use the bus for work – you can't get a full day in. You'll have to get a bike as far as the train, and leave your bike there. That's what most men do, it's only eight miles after all. Unless you can afford a car.'

I replied, 'No such luck. Our small savings will have to be used for some furniture, when we get settled.'

She shrugged. 'You'll sort something out I expect. If you've finished, I'll take the tray. Shan't see you in the morning, you'll be gone long before I'm around.'

We thanked her and said 'Goodnight' and she clumped away. As soon as we were alone, Ron said, 'Why didn't you eat your dinner? It wasn't too bad; anyway, I was starving.' His face was a picture when I told him why. I couldn't help laughing. 'I'm sorry, I couldn't tell you, she was standing right beside you.'

We washed and went to bed, brushing the cockroaches from the mattress and pulling the mosquito nets close. Vivienne was so deeply asleep that we left her as she was, unwashed and fully clothed.

Tired as I was, I lay awake a long time in the squalid room, staring into the darkness and listening to the insects clicking and buzzing, Ron's words echoing in my head.

'What on earth have I brought you to?'

What indeed?

Chapter 4

The Best-Laid Schemes

'You lazy bloody slut. Get up and get my breakfast!'

'For Heaven's sake, leave off. I was up first yesterday. Get yourself off today. And don't shout at me, you'll wake the kids.'

'Wake the bloody kids! Me! You shout like an old fishwife. Go. Get out of this bed.'

We sat up, startled. The noise was coming from below; the shouting increased, the language became obscene. There was a crash as if someone had thrown a plate against the wall and there were scuffles and bumps as if the pair were actually fighting. A child's frightened voice cried out, 'Mum, Mum, what are you doing?'

It was still dark and I felt as if I had only been asleep a few minutes. Ron's watch showed it was four a.m. and evidently Jean's husband was not at his best in the mornings. The noise continued for another few minutes or so, the children joining in, then, with a slam of their door and Jean's voice shrieking, 'Sod off, you miserable bastard!' peace was restored. Jimmy had apparently cycled off on his journey to work.

I was fully awake and somewhat alarmed at this exchange beneath us.

'Do you think they are always like this?' I asked Ron.

'Probably. I imagine that is the usual morning procedure; sounds as if neither likes getting up in the mornings.'

'I thought it was someone in our room when I woke up. I wonder why she doesn't pack his sandwiches overnight and save all the arguments.'

I had a sinking feeling that this so-called 'flat' was not going to be our home for very long.

25

'We might as well get up ourselves now. If we have to be outside by six
a.m., we need to allow plenty of time.' Ron got out of bed as he
spoke.

We washed and dressed and I put the kettle on the stove to boil for a cup
of tea. By the time Vivienne was awake and ready for the day we were at the
table with a piece of bread and margarine apiece, and still waiting for the
kettle to boil. An hour later, we were still waiting – the water was barely
lukewarm. Evidently the stove wasn't in very good working order. The
other ring on the hotplate didn't work at all. We settled for half a cup of
milk each. It was tepid and slightly sour, but it was better than no drink at
all. My longed-for hot cup of tea seemed remote.

We went out into the bright morning to await the arrival of the bus and
stood by the dusty dirt road watching the unfamiliar brilliant birds as they
darted in and out of the trees. A couple of hundred yards away we could see
the Pacific Ocean, the surf thundering onto the white sands. Swarms of tiny
sand flies crawled over us, minute creatures, up our nostrils and into our
eyes, so we had to swat each other with a broken twig to ward them off.
They bit, viciously, and we were relieved when the old, battered bus
arrived.

It was a rough journey, going a roundabout route, calling at all the small
villages to pick up the children on their way to school. They all carried
sandwich boxes and were barefoot. Not one was wearing any kind of
footwear. We reached Brisbane soon after nine o'clock and decided to
spend a few precious shillings on a breakfast. Hot tea and toasted sandwiches had never tasted so good. We hired an old wooden pushchair for the
day, knowing that there would be quite a lot of walking to do, and Valerie
would have an asthma attack if she began to tire. We had intended to go to
the bank first, draw some money and buy some stores, then go to the
Commonwealth Employment Bureau for Ron to register for work. Queen
Street in Brisbane is a street of banks, all of which over the next few days we
were to become more than familiar with.

No one had ever heard of us! Our nest egg of two hundred and fifty
pounds, which was a fortune to us, and should have been awaiting us, had
not arrived. We thought perhaps we had mistaken the name of the bank, so
we would try some of the others. So many of them had similar names, like
National Bank of Australia, The Australian National Bank, The Bank of
Australasia, etc. We tried them all. We trailed from bank to bank, growing
more despondent by the minute. The clerks who dealt with us were not in
the least interested; no money had been deposited in any of the banks in our
name and that was that. They suggested we should try again the next day.

Suddenly, it seemed, it was almost four o'clock. If we didn't catch the bus back to the Point, we would have to hitch a lift. We had achieved nothing.

The next two days the pattern was repeated: a diet of bread and marge, a cup of tea if we remembered to put only a small amount of water in the kettle and allow an hour and a half for it to boil, catch the bus to town and visit all the banks again. At the end of the third day we were desperate. Our money had almost gone and although I had sent an air letter to my parents asking them to contact our bank and find out what the problem was, we could not expect an answer for at least two weeks. No one was in the least helpful and through continual walking we both had painful blisters on our heels. It was the last straw when we missed the one and only bus back to the Point.

At this moment, as we saw it lurch away in a cloud of dust, the hired pushchair suddenly collapsed. As it crashed it trapped Vivienne's fingers, squashing three of them. To this day I can remember every detail of this incident. We extricated her and stood her on her feet. She started to cry and something in me snapped.

'Stop that!' I yelled. 'We haven't got time for you to cry. Shut up!'

The poor child did shut up, frightened into silence. Ron wrapped his handkerchief round her bleeding fingers and hoisted her on to his shoulders while I returned the wrecked pushchair to the hire shop. We started on our journey, trying to hitch a lift from any likely looking vehicle. We had no success at first, and had left the city far behind us, limping along the dirt roads into the country, when a truck pulled up beside us. Heaven sent, he was going all the way to the Point. We climbed in, exhausted, and dozed the journey away. The driver was delivering stores to the one small shop there. He set us down and Ron thanked him. He told him we could not afford to pay him for our lift but we would be pleased if he would accept a carton of cigarettes, bought duty–free on the ship. He was a jolly man and only accepted the gift when we begged him to. I think he must have said something about our plight to the lady who kept the shop for, as we walked towards our 'flat', she ran after us. She was carrying a huge fish!

'Would you like this?' She offered it to me.

'I haven't much money left. How much is it?'

'Go on, take it. I can shout you a fish. Go on, here.'

She pushed it into my hands and I took it, thankfully. Such small incidents helped to restore my faith in human nature.

While the fish was cooking, slowly, so slowly, we bathed Vivienne's crushed fingers and bound them up with clean white rag and Germolene from the small first aid kit I always kept. We washed the dust from ourselves and Ron and I soaked our feet in cold water, to ease the pain of our many blisters. We discussed our situation gloomily.

'What on earth are we going to do?' I asked.

'Let's think positively first. How much money have we left?'

We spread the remaining coins on the table before us. There was just enough to pay the single fare into Brisbane the next day. Nothing for food, not even the few coppers needed to hire a pushchair again. Our landlord had demanded a month's rent, for the time he said he had been saving the 'flat' for us. We had explained that we would pay when our money arrived from England. Although he wasn't very pleased about it, he had to accept our situation. After all, he couldn't have what we hadn't got! Privately, we thought he would have had a job to let the rooms anyway. It was no good asking Jimmy and Jean. Their morning fights continued and it was obvious that their financial position was little better than ours.

'Right, this is what we are going to do.' Ron put the coins into a little pile. 'Tomorrow, we are going into Brisbane again. We'll try the banks once more; the money might be there now. If it isn't, then we must go to the Department of Immigration and ask their help. Perhaps they will find us a room in town, then I can seek work. They might even lend us a few pounds to tide us over.'

'Well, we certainly can't go on like this. There is no way you are going to get a job while we are here. We have no choice really but to ask for help. They wouldn't let us starve, would they?' I didn't feel very confident about that.

Having made our decision, we turned our attention to food. The fish was ready, we put the kettle on the ring to make a pot of tea, cut our remaining piece of stale bread into three chunks and divided the strange-looking fish. It was a feast!

The round of banks next day told the same old story – no money, no letters from our bank in England, stalemate. At the last bank on our list Ron asked to see the manager. He wasn't available, but the under-manager would give us a few moments of his time. At last we would see someone in a position of authority. We told him our tale of woe and threw ourselves on his mercy. He was quite helpful.

'I can't lend you any money, of course,' he said. 'You have no proper address, even, no job and no references, but I can cable your bank in England. The cost of a cable will be several pounds, if you will sign an undertaking to reimburse us when the money arrives. Give it several days. In fact, if we say this time next week, I am confident the matter will be resolved.'

This was a glimmer of hope, so we signed the form provided, thanked him and left. The next port of call was the Immigration Office, to the employment room first, to see what kind of job Ron could obtain. Vivienne and I waited outside and when the interview was over and Ron emerged I could see by his expression that he had not been successful.

'No luck?'

'Oh yes, they offered me a job all right – maintenance on a railway track.'

'Well, it would be something to start with, you have worked on the railways before and you don't mind manual work.' I tried to sound encouraging.

'It wasn't that simple, the job was several hundred miles away! I would be one of a gang working on the track, living in a tent alongside the line, for three months at a time. At the end of three months they would fly us back to the city for a week's leave, then back to wherever we were needed. It would mean that you and Vivienne would have to stay here, and I'm not prepared to do that. After all, we haven't even got anywhere to live yet.' He sounded bitter.

'What now, then?'

'They have agreed to give us a meal, then at two o'clock I have to report to another office where our situation will be discussed. You had better come with me to that one. After that, who knows?'

It was while we were seated at a long trestle table in a Nissen hut, awaiting our free meal, that we had a stroke of luck. Seated opposite we recognised a family who had been fellow passengers on the *Orsova*. They were with a number of other families, all of whom were going into the northern part of Queensland, and were to be flown up the next day. After our meal we walked in the garden with them. They had three small children and an elderly father travelling with them. They had been housed in a hostel since arriving and were anxious to complete their journey. We told them what had happened to us and they insisted on lending us five pounds. Wonderful! We made a note of their address, unable to give them ours, as we had no idea where we might be. Weeks later, when I was able to return the loan we had a nice letter from Rosemary. They had not settled at all well – her eighty-year-old father could not stand the climate, so they were looking for a position somewhere cooler. We never heard from them again but often wondered how they fared.

Our two o'clock appointment was harrowing. The official was not in the least interested in us or our problems. He told us curtly that they were not a 'Lending Department' and that as Ron had turned down the one job they were obliged to offer, we were 'on our own'. He did, however, direct us to yet another office. They dealt with the housing problems and they might be able to tell us of a vacant room. Not very promising!

The housing office was in another hut some distance from the other buildings, set in a pretty landscaped garden. Vivienne and I decided to wait on a seat outside, in the warm sunshine. Another young woman was already sitting there. She smiled at us and said 'Good afternoon' in a marked foreign accent. She had a pleasant round face, straight brown hair and gold–rimmed glasses. Ron came out in a few moments, holding a piece of paper, stamped with an official-looking stamp.

'We have this address to go to. If the room is still to let we must come back and let them know if we are taking it. They will arrange transport for us, probably for tomorrow morning.'

I jumped up. 'Good, that sounds a bit more hopeful.'

Ron referred to the paper. 'We can get a tram outside the gates; we ask for stop 132. The house is at 168 Albion Road.'

'And dat will be six peoples to share one kitchen!'

'I beg your pardon?' The voice from the seat was unfriendly, gone was the smile.

'I live dere too. Ve had been outback vorking, now mine husband is looking for vork in de city, and ve haf a room in dat house.'

I felt uncomfortable; it wasn't a good start.

'Well, we can go and look at the room anyway, it may not be suitable.' We turned away and left her staring after us. It was quite a long ride on the bumpy tramcar. We had to break into our precious five pounds to pay our fares. As we rattled along towards the outer suburbs, Ron muttered, 'What a start, homeless, jobless and practically penniless.'

I said, 'It can only get better from now on, then, can't it?'

I received a grunt in reply. The house was on the main road, opposite our stop. It was one-storied, built of wood and asbestos, with a corrugated iron roof. Like its neighbours, it stood on high stilts. Palm trees grew in the dusty garden and it had an air of neglect about it. A rotting verandah ran round the side and the front door stood open. We knocked and a plump-faced Scots girl answered.

'We have come to see if the room is still vacant.' Ron held out the paper for her to see.

'Come in, no one has taken it yet,' she said. 'My name is Betty. The landlord is a teacher, he is away on a month's special course. So I am in charge!' She had a broad Scots accent. 'Come away in.' She stood aside and we entered a dim passage. She indicated rooms leading off, either side.

'A young Dutch couple live there. They have only been there a few days,

Hans and Corrie. He hasn't got work yet. A girl from Yugoslavia lives here, a proper glamour girl is Lisa, but nice with it,' with a wink to Ron. She opened the next door.

'This is our room, bit of a muddle and rather dark, as you can see. But it's not too bad, better than the last place we had. Gets a bit crowded, what with my husband, Dick and the two kids.' The room was poorly furnished with just the basic needs.

The fourth door she opened led into a very dark room. We soon saw why. The only window looked out into a verandah room that had been fitted with glass louvres.

'Albert and Margie Woods have this room. Isn't it awful, no proper furniture, just that old stretcher bed and those two broken chairs. It was all they could afford. He is blind so he doesn't know how awful it is; poor old Margie does the best she can.'

I felt sorry for the unknown Margie. Betty went on, 'They are Australians, come up from Melbourne, can't think why. They have gone out for a walk now.'

The room that served as a lounge had several more rooms leading from it: a small one which Mr Church, the owner, occupied, a kitchen with a yellow stone sink, a gas stove, a deal table and an enormous fridge.

'We all share this kitchen,' Betty explained. 'It is difficult as there are only four gas rings and the oven, so that's one ring for each family and one can use the oven. We do have a kind of rota, when it works.' She laughed as she said it and I thought of the saying that two women can't share one kitchen. What about six women then? I remembered the girl at the Immigration Department, who no doubt was already finding out the problems, which I would soon share.

At the other end of the lounge was a lobby which led to the bathroom and the room we were to have. It was a real bathroom, with a washbasin and a flush toilet. Our room opened off the lobby, a large but rather dark room, but a definite improvement on the 'flat'. A long flight of steps led from the back of the lounge down to the garden. Under the house were a few sheets of asbestos nailed around the supports. Betty gestured toward it. 'Old Mary lives under there. She talks to herself all the time. She will scuttle up and down when she wants to use the kitchen or bathroom; it's not very often though. Don't know how she manages most of the time for the toilet and so on, but there, that's her problem. Well, what do you think of it?'

'We'll take it.' We both spoke at once. It was fairly central and although shabby and poorly furnished, it was much cleaner than the 'flat'.

Ron said, 'We do have some trouble though. At the moment we can't pay any rent.' Once again we told our story. This time the reaction was quite different.

'That's OK. Mr Church won't be back for almost a month. By then your money will have arrived, and you will get some sort of a job.'

So it was agreed, we would take up residence the next day. As we travelled back to the city, I found myself hoping we would all get on together. Fourteen people, all to share one kitchen and one bathroom, one cooker and one sink. We would certainly need to be tolerant. We arranged with the housing officer about our transport for the morrow, signed an agreement to pay back the cost when our money arrived, and were just in time to catch the bus back to the point. Today we could pay our fare, and we had food for a meal. Things were looking up.

While we waited for our transport the next morning we went down to explain to Jean why we were moving. She did not invite us into her abode, and I could quite see why. Like the shack at the Albion Road house, Jean's was also a few sheets of asbestos, nailed round the supports, with a dirt floor. There were a number of nails in the posts, on which were hanging an assortment of clothes. A couple of old iron bedsteads were bent into the spaces between the posts, and the place reeked of old meals, grease and dirt. It was so dark it was impossible to see any other furniture they might have had. I couldn't imagine anyone staying there.

Perhaps it was understandable that they quarrelled so much, and with three growing children, life could not have been easy. She was offended that we were leaving, going on at length about the difficulty she had had in persuading Mr Dawson to save the 'flat' for us, and so on, reminding us how much money we owed him, etcetera. We parted on a very sour note. The truck was due at ten a.m. It arrived at six thirty, by which time it was almost dusk. We hadn't eaten anything since breakfast, as we had expected the truck at any moment, so we were, once again, hungry. We loaded up and were away into the growing darkness. 'Like nomads we are,' I said. 'It seems months since we had a proper home of our own.'

'Never mind, next time we move it will be to a real house of our own.' Ron sounded more optimistic than he had for days. By the time we reached Albion Road, it was completely dark and all the night insects were out in full flight. The house was silent, the occupants no doubt at their evening meals and the children in bed. We took possession of our room, though our trunks and bedding boxes were still in transit somewhere *en route* from Sydney. Like the 'flat', no bedding was supplied. There were two beds in the room, a double one and a small camp bed. An old eiderdown, a couple of grubby pillows and one blanket were lying there, left by a former occupant,

I thought. So, with a coat and a dressing gown we made up the beds. There was a ricketty table, one leg propped up by a book, four kitchen chairs and two ancient armchairs with the stuffing falling out, a chest of drawers and a bookshelf. An alcove was curtained off as a wardrobe.

'We can make this quite homely when our trunks arrive,' I said. 'Hang a few pictures over those damp patches and wash those filthy curtains.' My spirits rose.

Ron said, 'It's quiet too, now the traffic has died down a bit.' He spoke too soon. Albert and Margie had arrived home. Their bed groaned as someone sat on it. 'My bloody feet are killing me,' a woman's voice roared. The voice was so close it was as if they were in our room.

'I'm going to the bog, Albert.' A door opened, footsteps thumped across the lounge, the lobby door slammed and Margie entered the bathroom. I won't go into details; suffice it to say that we would certainly know whether any occupant of the 'little' room was going to make a long or a short stay! As the toilet roll rattled down we burst out laughing. I had to cover my face to stifle the noise.

'The walls must be cardboard,' Ron spluttered. The noise of the cistern made me look to see if the water was coming through the wall. One thing I was sure of, whatever life was going to be like in Albion Road, it wasn't going to be dull!

Chapter 5

Almost a Family

My surmise that life in Albion Road would certainly not be dull was correct. What an odd assortment of people we were. Hans and Corrie had been in the country almost a year, having left Holland the day after their marriage. Hans was a carpenter and had been offered a job doing what was known as 'bush carpentry'. Miles from anywhere, they had been employed by a cattle farmer, Hans to do the many jobs needed on a large station: new barns, fences, extra bunk houses for the hired hands and so on, Corrie to work in the house. They were given room and board and a small wage in return for their labour. It had been a very lonely life and a hard one. Hans probably had the better time as most of his work was outdoors, while Corrie had been under the eagle eye of the farmer's wife, always confined to the house. Outside, the tiny flies were a pest, also the mosquitoes, and a hat with veil and dangling corks was a necessity, as depicted in so many outback cartoons. Indoors, the heat was unbearable and in the daytime the humidity was so high that Corrie found it almost impossible to do her set tasks. She frequently got up in the night to do the laundry. Like most of the houses a laundry room was situated beneath the house, not really a room but two stone troughs and a tap. A large brick copper was used to boil the clothes, the fire being fed with wood chips and small logs. The clothes were then scrubbed in the troughs with the aid of an old-fashioned washboard, in the same fashion that our grandmothers had operated.

Unhappy as they were with their circumstances, they had to stay the term of their contract, though that nine months must have seemed like twice as long. At the end of the time, they decided to try their luck in Brisbane and, although they had found the room to rent, Hans had as yet to find employment. Corrie was terribly homesick and we always knew when she had received a letter from her family. The walls were so thin, only a single sheet of plywood, that whatever was said or done in one room was quite audible in the rooms adjoining. Whenever a letter had arrived from Holland, Hans and Corrie would stay in their room instead of joining the crowd in the lounge for the evening. We could hear them singing mournful Dutch songs and clapping their hands in time to the melody. We were all homesick so we shared their feelings.

Lisa was a lovely blonde from Yugoslavia, about twenty-five years old. She, with her parents, two young brothers and a married sister and brother-in-law, had been in Australia for ten months. In their own country they had been wealthy. Lisa's father had owned several factories and the pictures of their home and its surroundings were beautiful. During the Tito régime they had been forced to flee, allowed to take only the few possessions they could carry. For some time they had been housed in a refugee camp in Austria, finally being accepted for resettlement in Australia, although they were still 'stateless persons'. One of the conditions of their residence was that they must work for at least a year in any job to which they were directed. Lisa had been sent to Brisbane to work as a domestic in a large mental hospital, while her family were still in Sydney. Her father and brother-in-law were factory hands, her two young brothers were still at school and her mother was permitted, for health reasons, to stay at home. Her elder sister was expecting her first child. She received every attention, for her child would, of course, be a 'New Australian'. At the end of three years they would be able to apply for citizenship. This was a great grief for Lisa – she hated the thought of giving up her own nationality, at the same time realising that they would never be able to go back to their country. Her work in the hospital was hard and far from congenial but she had no choice. She tried to make the best of it and attended evening classes, as did Hans and Corrie, to master English. I was full of admiration for them, they learnt so quickly. We all liked Lisa, always cheerful and full of fun. She ate no meat or fish and cooked the most interesting things for her evening meals, filling the house with tantalising savoury smells that were the envy of us all.

Dick and Betty, with four-year-old Penny and William, who was nearly two, were from a rural part of Scotland. Dick had always worked on a farm and was finding it hard to adjust to life in a town. He was a pleasant if somewhat feckless young man. Like Hans and Corrie, they had been sent to a job on a cattle station in Northern Queensland, Dick employed in caring for the animals and Betty to work in the house. When she found herself pregnant with their third child, the work had been too heavy and the farmer's wife had made it clear that no allowances would be made, so they would have to seek another position. They had booked a flight to Brisbane and sent their belongings back by carrier truck. The plane had been a small one and the flight turbulent. Betty had gone into labour and actually lost the baby during the flight. As she was five months pregnant, it had been a traumatic experience and, although she had recovered physically, she was in a highly nervous condition. The fact that Dick had not yet found work made things worse and their relationship was at a low ebb. Dick had developed an interest in horse racing which was one of the most popular entertainments there. Most of his time was spent at the racecourse, and, after he obtained work, most of his wages too!

It was not unusual for Dick to go off to the 'Trotting Races' as the evening meetings were called, and lose his entire week's wages. We grew to dread Friday nights. There would be a terrible quarrel between Betty and Dick and he would storm out of the house to spend what little he had left at the pub across the road, leaving Betty in tears with no money left for food or rent. The rest of us would have a whip-round. Between us we had very little but if we couldn't put money in the kitty, we contributed food.

Little Mary, who lived under the house, was the one person we never really got to know. She scuttled up and down, as Betty had told us, chattering away to herself in such a broad Australian accent that we never knew what she was talking about. I don't believe Mr Church did either. I think he inherited Mary along with the house. He didn't know who she really was or where she came from, only that she had been there for years. I suppose as long as she paid her rent and was no trouble, he wasn't bothered anyway.

Mr Church himself was a small man with an impish sense of humour. He lived in his tiny room and cooked for himself but always joined us in the lounge after the evening meal. He had been married once but, apart from referring to 'My Ex' occasionally, we knew nothing about his life. In term time he was out all day and weekends often went away, so he didn't trouble us at all. I think he quite enjoyed having a house full of such diverse characters, to say nothing of enjoying the money it brought him. Six rents coming in each week must have been very welcome.

Margie and Albert Wood were the oddest pair of all. He was well over six feet tall, very thin and completely blind. He attended a centre for the blind each day and was taken to and fro by taxi. Margie was enormous, as tall as Albert and weighing all of eighteen stone. Her arms would not have disgraced a stevedore and her bosom was beyond belief! I have never, before or since, seen one of such ample proportions. Albert was as quiet as she was noisy and her language was colourful, to say the least. Their dark little room must have been a nightmare; with the bed, two chairs and the pair of them in it, there could have been little room to move. Margie acquired two orange boxes which she adapted as a table and store cupboard which crowded the room even more. In spite of her size, she was a superb cook and would bake dainty cakes and the lightest of pastry. In the mornings she worked in a restaurant and in the afternoons would literally take over the kitchen to prepare her evening meal. In theory, we were supposed to work on a rota basis for the use of the stove: one person to each gas ring and one to use the oven and the sixth person to wait until the others had finished. In practice it didn't work.

Margie would instal herself at the deal table, spread her equipment all round and roar, 'I don't care which of youse buggers turn it is, I'm here and here I stay. Youse all can wait until I'm through.'

I think we were somewhat in awe of her for no one ever argued. Margie also took a great fancy to my husband. When he eventually managed to obtain more permanent work as a builder's labourer, as had Dick and Hans, all working for the same firm, they travelled to and from work together, returning at about six thirty each evening. Dick and Hans would slip quietly into their rooms on their return, leaving Ron to run the gauntlet. He would creep down the passage, hoping to reach the safety of our room without the dreaded Margie's nightly assault. As he had to pass through the lounge on the way, she was always lying in wait. No matter how quiet he was, she heard him. She would leave the kitchen, sail across the room and grab him as he came through the doorway. Enfolding him in her huge arms, she would crush him to her bosom, where he would literally disappear. Considering he is five feet eleven inches tall and weighs twelve stone, this was no mean feat. She would cry, 'How's me darlin' then, how's his day bin then?'

He would come up gasping for air, his arms flailing like the sails of a windmill. I was too helpless with laughter to go to his aid. He used to say to me, 'Can't you try to see that she is elsewhere when I come home?' And deprive me of a little entertainment!

The first two weeks of our stay in Albion Road we had a struggle to manage. The five pounds loaned to us by Rosemary had soon been used and once again we were without food. At this time I didn't know our fellow occupants well enough to ask for their help but I found a useful source of revenue. Milk bottles and jam jars were returnable, a few coppers for each.

Underneath the house I found a heap of filthy bottles which I was able to wash and return to the dairy. The money I received was enough to purchase some groceries for a couple of meals. Neighbouring hedges and gateways yielded a daily harvest and in this way we were able to eat, albeit on a very economical scale.

The first job that Ron found was temporary, shovelling coke at a gas works. It was back-breaking, dirty work, but it lasted for ten days, straight off, including a Saturday and Sunday. When he returned to the Employment Bureau at the end of the job, they were amazed. The clerk called his colleagues to see Ron, as if he were a zoological specimen – apparently no one lasted more than a day at the gas works. On the strength of this they sent him to the building site where Dick and Hans subsequently were able to join him.

Our money eventually arrived at The Bank of Australia and we found out that the long delay had been the fault of our bank in England. They had forgotten to send it to us! Needless to say, we have never used that bank since for all the hassle they caused us. I would not recommend them to anyone, even if I do enjoy their Black Horse commercials! We settled all our debts, which made a staggering hole in our nest egg, and gradually we became used to our new way of life.

The evenings were a source of great entertainment. About five thirty the fun would begin. The licensing hours in Australia were totally different from ours at home. They varied from state to state and in Queensland it was from six a.m. to six p.m. The public house opposite was beside the tram stop, where the homegoing workers would pour from the vehicle, straight into the door for what was known as the six o'clock swill.

The object of the exercise seemed to be the swallowing of as many pints of liquid as possible in the short space of time before the bar closed. Women were not allowed in bars at that period, so it was men only. As soon as the bar was crowded, they formed queues on the pavement outside, making it hazardous for anyone trying to pass. Hairy arms protruded from all the open windows, passing out foaming glasses to the eager waiting hands. It was a sight to be seen, all these men clamouring for a drink as if it might be their last! The passers-by dodged in and out of the cars and the trams rattled along on their tracks in the centre of the road, taking it all as a matter of course, while we on the verandah found it quite a diversion.

After our evening meal we would gather in the lounge, swapping stories of our varied adventures and our homelands. Later in the evening one of us would go into the kitchen and make a large pot of tea, to be shared among us. This always provided one of the highlights of our life. Not the tea, but the stampede of cockroaches as soon as the kitchen light was turned on. They would swarm in all directions, under the fridge or the skirting boards or beneath the sink cupboard. They were huge brown creatures, some of them three inches long. We would rush to stamp on them and no sooner did they lie dead than the ants would appear, columns of them marching across the floor. Each group would carve up a corpse and march away again, every ant carrying his own particular joint of meat. Across the broken lino the empty brown shells would rock gently to and fro like so many little boats on a windy sea. The whole procedure took only a few moments and could be repeated as many times as we wished. We never succeeded in eradicating the cockroaches or any of the hoards of insects that shared our lives. Mr Church would sit by, protesting mildly, 'They are all right, really; after all, they do live here!'

With no money to spare, paid-for entertainment was out of the question but we certainly found plenty to laugh about. There was a nightly queue for the bathroom and toilet but eventually we would settle down for the night. Well, almost all of us. As I have said, the walls were so thin that we could only converse in whispers in our rooms. If we spoke aloud, we could hold conversations with each other as we lay in bed – it was rather like all sleeping together. The beds were really old, just wooden stretchers with wire coils across. The mattresses were horse-hair, so lumpy that it was like sleeping on a bag of golf balls. We tried to turn our mattress once but all the horse hair fell out on the floor and we had to stuff it back in again.

The bed in Margie's room was smaller than the others, and of course it took up most of their room. Their routine never varied. They were always the last to go to bed. There was a tremendous creaking as Margie's bulk descended on the protesting springs, then she would shriek, 'Move over, Albert, that bloody horse-hair's sticking up my arse again!'

He would groan, 'Don't do that, Margie, don't do it, please Margie, don't —' then CRASH as he hit the floor. The rest of us, weak with laughter, would bang on the partitions, calling out, 'Leave him alone, you great bully, give him a hand back into bed,' and similar advice. Poor old Albert, he had much to put up with. Being blind, he stood no chance against the monstrous Margie. We often wondered how they came to be together, the gentle quiet Albert and the coarse, noisy but nevertheless good-hearted Margie.

No, life in Albion Street was never dull, and our 'almost a family' a source of unfailing interest.

Chapter 6

My Teeth and I

It was during the next month or two that I began to suffer from severe toothache. This was no surprise to me at all as all my life my teeth have been a nuisance, but this time there was a different reason. This was no ordinary toothache. I visited several dentists in the city, all of whom told me the same reasons for my problem. My four wisdom teeth were impacted, growing around the lower jawbone. There was no way any of them would touch my teeth. As one of the dentists said, 'It's a hammer and chisel job – couldn't possibly be done in the surgery. I'll make arrangements for you to have an X-ray at the Dental Hospital.'

The X-rays highlighted the diagnosis: eight teeth would have to be extracted, about three days in hospital, a mouthful of stitches until the gums healed, absolutely nothing to it, so they assured me. Nothing to it! They didn't know my teeth like I did. I duly received a letter asking me to present myself at the Brisbane General Hospital one Thursday afternoon. In Australia at that time there was no National Health Service and any medical treatment was very expensive. The only free hospital in the country was, in fact, the Brisbane General. It was funded by a lottery known as the Golden Casket. Lotteries, and for that matter any form of gambling, were popular, and on many street corners were small booths selling tickets. The prizes were generous and all excess monies went to the upkeep of the hospital. People came from all over the state to take advantage of the facilities, which meant that it was always crowded. However, I was grateful that I, too, would be able to use the service.

I was asked to take an overnight bag and report to the reception office at two p.m. I left Vivienne with Corrie, as Ron was at work, and caught the bus to the hospital. It was an enormous complex of buildings and Nissen huts, stretching along a high bank, overlooking a busy main road on the outskirts of the city. No one in the main office seemed to have any idea of my admission or, for that matter, of the location of the dental ward. I was sent from building to building, with no success until, at last, a passing nurse told me they did not have an actual dental ward. Dental cases were dealt with wherever there was a spare bed – it could be in any ward. It was two hours before I found myself in a small dark room and told to await the Sister, who would deal with me.

After a few moments, a young girl came in with her mother. She had a small case with her and seemed rather nervous.

'Am I in the right place?' she asked me. 'We have been trying for ages to find the dental ward. Tomorrow I am going to have all my teeth out. I dread it!'

I assured her she was in the right place and we had to wait for the Sister. Her mother left and we sat chatting. Her name was Melanie, she told me, she was terrified of hospitals and had never been in one before. She smiled nervously and I saw that all her teeth were just black stumps. I thought it such a shame that a pretty girl like Melanie would be toothless by this time tomorrow.

Sister finally appeared and took us through into an adjoining room, furnished like a surgery. She asked us for details of any previous operations, or any medical condition which might be relevant. She then opened a cupboard and produced two stainless steel bedpans, each covered with a white cloth.

'Into those cubicles, please,' she said briskly. 'A sample of urine from each of you.' She waved at a pair of curtained-off booths. Melanie and I emerged together, self-consciously clasping our pans. We looked at each other and then at our receptacles. The pristine cloth over hers had a large wet stain on it. Her eyes filled with tears. 'Oh dear, I though they wanted it strained!'

I howled with laughter, it looked so funny. Sister was not amused – it was not an auspicious start to our stay. Later that evening I went into the bathroom opening from our crowded ward and joined the group waiting to use the basins and toilets. A lady standing next to me had a tracheotomy tube protruding from her throat. She looked really ill and I said, 'Poor you, whatever have you had done?'

She spoke in a hoarse whisper, 'It's not as bad as it looks. I came in two weeks ago to have some teeth out. I don't know what went wrong but my windpipe was pierced. I've been here ever since.'

I sympathised with her and returned to my bed, dreading the morning.

Unable to sleep, I lay in the darkness, thinking back to my early childhood and reliving my various dental visits, growing more apprehensive by the minute.

My teeth have always been the most 'unfavourite' part of my anatomy. My sister, who is thirteen months my senior, has beautiful teeth; on her bi-annual visits to the dentist she rarely has to have as much as a filling. Most unfair! I think that the calcium or whatever it is that makes strong bones and teeth, must have been in short supply when I arrived. One of my earliest experiences of dentistry took place when I was about five years old. I remember the raging pain in my jaw, and my mother holding a bag of hot salt to my face. It evidently did not work, for after a day or two, she said,

'We are going to have to have a visit to the dentist, I'm afraid. We must catch a bus into Rye and get your tooth taken out. Unless you would let Auntie Win take it out for you. She could do it quite easily. If you are a good girl, I will give you sixpence!'

Riches indeed! I settled for the latter. I was taken to our outer wash-house, a brick-floored room with a large stone copper and a mangle, where every Monday it was a hive of activity, full of steam and several zinc baths with rinsing water and Reckitts Blue. Mother tied me into a chair, then she and my grandmother stood behind me, holding my head firmly, while my aunt produced a pair of pliers. Obediently I opened my mouth wide, my aunt gripped the offending molar, gave a twist and a tug, and it was all over! All over, that is, except for my sense of outrage as I spat blood, too shocked to cry. I got my sixpence, but in later years I often thought I must have saved my mother quite a lot of money. There would have been the bus fares to Rye, the dentist's fee and, no doubt, some refreshment while we awaited the return bus. And I got sixpence!

The second trip to a dentist was about a year later. We were in our house in Chatham, my father's home port, for a few months, and my sister and I were attending the local school. I was again suffering severe toothache and my mother had taken me to the clinic. It was a pink-washed building, standing on a high pavement in the main road. The smell that assailed my nostrils on entering haunts me still. I was to have 'gas' they told me. Strapped into an enormous brown leather chair, the nurse asked me to blow up a 'balloon'. She held something over my face and there was the dreadful smell again. I fought like a mad creature, hitting out with my arms and legs, trying to push the wretched thing away. The nurse and the dentist fought back, pushing me back, back into the chair. I remember him saying, 'For goodness sake hold her still, beastly child.' Suddenly, I was spinning away, into oblivion. I had the most awful dream. I was on a cart, being pushed along a road, very fast; there were people running alongside, trying to keep pace. The cart went faster and faster – I knew it would soon tip over. I was tied on and however I struggled I could not free myself. Faster and faster, and then, it tipped. I was flung up into the air, then someone was slapping my face, 'Wake up, wake up, here, spit in this bowl.'

I awoke, blood everywhere; the dentist, looking so angry, his white coat splashed with red, as if someone had tipped a bottle of tomato sauce on him. My mother was brought into the room and told how naughty I had been and that it was my own fault that I was bleeding so badly. White and shaking, I was taken home on the bus, a large handkerchief held to my face, becoming more bloody every second. My poor mother was accused by an angry man sitting opposite of 'letting someone butcher that child – what kind of mother are you?'

It continued like that all through my school days; at every dental inspection I needed filling or extractions. Off to the clinic I would go, clutching my pink card. I always went alone, unlike most of my contemporaries. I did not want anyone with me. Whatever pain or humiliation I was going to suffer, I would not be seen by friends or relations, only the dental staff.

Now, as a grown woman with a child of my own, I felt much the same. Alone, I had endured my night of painful memories, though finally I must have slept because I awoke in the narrow hospital bed – the moment I had dreaded had arrived!

There was no breakfast for Melanie or me, and just before nine a.m. a nurse came to give a pre-med injection. I was dressed in a short cotton gown, with tapes at the back, so short that it barely covered my requirements, long woollen stockings which reached the tops of my thighs, flannel slippers and the outfit completed with a white turban. Within a few moments the nurse reappeared carrying a clipboard and some papers which I presumed contained my medical notes. She told me to follow her and off we went.

On the rare occasions I have had to undergo surgery I have always been taken on a trolley. Not this time! I walked behind the erect starched figure, out of the hospital, in full view of the road, down a long and winding path, for what seemed miles. It was just as well that the injection had taken effect, or I should have felt the spectacle I undoubtedly looked!

The operating theatre must have been at the extreme edge of the grounds, and by the time we entered the long corridor leading to the theatre, my legs felt like jelly. The nurse thrust my notes into my hand, told me to wait until it was my turn and left me. Three hours later I was still sitting there, the injection had long ago worn off and I was only too conscious of my undignified appearance! I had watched a number of operations come and go and remembered thinking it was a good job I did not have a weak stomach! I tried to ask several people how much longer I was going to be kept waiting but all I got was a wave of the hand and the reply 'You'll be going in soon.' If I had been wearing my own clothes, I would have gone home; as it was, I had no choice but to sit there and try to be patient. It was after half–past twelve when I was at last taken into the theatre and given my anaesthetic, and I remembered no more until I woke up late that evening back in the ward.

I felt ghastly, my throat was raw and I was so thirsty. I asked for a drink but was brought instead a cup of ice cubes, this being the best thing, apparently, for stopping the bleeding. I could see Melanie further down the ward, fast asleep. I wondered how she had fared. When I staggered out to the bathroom much later, I had the shock of my life! I peered in the mirror and stared at myself in horror. Hammer and chisel job, the dentist had said! I looked as if I had just gone ten rounds with Henry Cooper! My face was already black and blue, the marks where the tubes had been in my nose and throat had left deep tram lines down my cheeks, and when I tried to speak I had no voice at all.

I was allowed home on the Sunday, still voiceless, where Ron had cooked a beautiful roast dinner which, of course, I could not eat. I existed for the next week on soup or mashed bananas, anything more solid refusing to go down.

I had an appointment two weeks later at the hospital, to have the stitches removed. Early on the morning of that day, I decided I could not face it so, with the aid of a small mirror and a pair of sharp nail scissors, I did the job myself. I kept the appointment and the surgeon seemed somewhat surprised that 'the stitches must have come out while I was eating'. He was pleased with the result of my operation and did not want to see me again. The feeling was mutual!

I can't help thinking: when we were created, why couldn't teeth have been like hair? When one hair drops out, another grows – why not teeth? It would have been a much better arrangement, especially for someone like me!

Chapter 7

Moving On

After I recovered from my short stay in hospital, Vivienne and I began to explore our surroundings. The weather, although winter, was warmer than an English summer with long golden days and occasional high winds but no rain. (The wet season in Queensland arrives in January or February and lasts for several weeks.) There was a lovely Botanical Garden in Brisbane where we would often take a picnic – a small menagerie attracted the children and the monkey enclosure acted like a magnet. The crowd in front of the various members of the ape family never seemed to grow smaller.

We also made friends with a couple of our own age who came from our home town. They had been in Australia almost four years; our mothers were, in fact, near neighbours. Although we had never met Phillip and Joy we had written to each other. When we were seeking a sponsor, I had obtained their address and sent a letter asking if they were able to offer us any advice. Joy had replied – one of the cautious answers – saying that they were not really able to help us in any way. We realised that they were living in a small settlement about thirty miles from the city, so contacted them and arranged to visit them. Ron was at work but Vivienne and I caught a train and Joy met us at the small siding that served as a station. It was a rather barren-looking area and their home was a garage. Made of asbestos with a concrete floor, it was one of a small estate. This was quite a usual procedure: a plot of land could be purchased for a few hundred pounds, a garage or a verandah erected, and a family could move in until they could afford to build a proper house. All too often the house was never built, financial circumstances preventing it. Many families lived like this until their children were grown up. Sometimes, the dwelling was just a large shed, known as a Humpy, and in time we grew accustomed to seeing these and knew a number of the occupants. There was usually a large American-type car outside and often an enormous fridge. They seemed to be the top priorities – a car for transport to and from work, a fridge for keeping the beer cold. No one worried about such minor items as a kitchen sink or a toilet!

Phillip and Joy's garage was well built and immaculate inside, simply but adequately furnished. A strong hen-house with some healthy looking hens and a vegetable plot were outside and a toilet stood at the end of the garden. It had a 'Dry Pan' as they called it. The 'night cart' called once a week, in the daytime actually, leaving a clean pan in place of the used one and a box of sawdust and wood shavings to sprinkle on the contents each time it was used. Joy told me that at night when they visited the toilet, they had to share it with a number of bright green frogs who climbed up the walls and could be seen in the beam of their torchlight, peering through the small window.

I asked Joy why she had sent me such a cautious reply to my letter. Her answer surprised me. 'I found it very difficult to know what to say. If I had told you that we are booked to go home, I would have had to find reasons for you.'

'Do you mean you really are booked to go home?'

'Yes, in December. We have never really settled, the climate doesn't suit me and we don't feel that this is where we want to spend the rest of our lives. You might love it out here, but if I had told you we were leaving, it could have sown seeds of doubt in your minds. Then, if you hadn't come, you would have always wondered if you had done the right thing.'

I could see her point. No one can make up another person's mind for them, but I was sorry to think that my new-found friends would soon be leaving. Many times over the next two years I found myself in the same situation as Joy had been, and I, too, would write a cautious letter to a would-be immigrant. Phillip and Joy became very good friends of ours during the next few months, a friendship which is still as strong as ever. We live only six miles distant from them and visit each other frequently.

They sold their garage and took rooms just round the corner from Albion Road, while they were waiting to sail. We often spent our Sundays together, visiting places of interest. Phillip was a talented artist and always carried his sketch-pad, making quick notes and drawings of places he wanted to paint at a later date. One lovely Sunday we went to a local beauty spot called

Lone Pine Sanctuary. It was high on a hill, thickly studded with a variety of trees. Mainly they were eucalyptus and they housed a colony of koala bears. The animals were able to roam freely and the only ones enclosed were the females about to produce young.

Very few buses went up to the sanctuary and we were toiling up the steep hill when a large black car pulled up. 'Want a lift?' enquired the driver. He lived in the area and told us he was going to the top of the hill. We accepted and climbed in thankfully. Within seconds we were wishing we hadn't! He was an appalling driver, telling us proudly that he was seventy-six and had only passed his driving test the week before! The road wound round the mountain side and a cliff fell away sheer to one side. Several times he missed his gear and twice went into reverse, backing towards the edge, so that we were looking down the cliff face. I could almost see the headlines in the next day's paper: 'POMMIES KILLED IN CLIFF TRAGEDY'.

At one stage, we passed a squashed possum. 'Killed that on the way down,' he told us cheerfully. A little later, 'See that broken fence, went through there on Wednesday; good job it wasn't on the other side!' He laughed, we didn't. Halfway up the hill the car was making a dreadful noise and black smoke was pouring out of the exhaust.

'Can't understand why she's not pulling,' he muttered.

'Could be because you've got the handbrake on,' Phillip said dryly – he was sitting in the front passenger seat.

'So I have.' A crunch and we were off again, grinding upward. It was the most hair-raising ride of our lives. At one point, Joy said, 'Thank you very much for our lift; we mustn't trouble you any more, we will walk the rest of the way.'

'Certainly not, I'll get you to the top, if it's the last thing I do,' he insisted.

'Probably will be the last thing any of us do,' Ron whispered.

We reached the top finally and got out, our legs still shaking. With a wave and a screech of tyres, he left us, roaring off down the hill. Hours later, when we returned by bus, we watched for signs of a large, wrecked, black car. We didn't see one and agreed that he must have a guardian angel working overtime!

In spite of the traumatic ride, the visit was a worthwhile experience. The little bears were enchanting; we were allowed to nurse one of the residents of the maternity wing. With one hand under its rump and its arms clasped round my neck, the warm creature nestled against me, smelling faintly of oil of eucalyptus. We were told they never have any lice and are some of the cleanest animals alive. One mother bear came close enough for us to see her baby. It peeped out of her pouch, no bigger than a fieldmouse, the first time it had been seen and it was known to be already six months old. Altogether a day to remember.

At the house Corrie and I became good companions; she was very lonely and we spent a lot of time together, going for walks and picnics. Although she and Hans had mastered the language very well, they seemed unsettled and it was no surprise to us when they told us that they had booked a passage back to Holland and would sail in September.

'I just can't stand the insects,' she told me, 'especially the cockroaches. To think that they get into our drawers and are on my underwear,' she shuddered.

I agreed. I found it hard to get used to as well. Each night, when we went to bed, we had to make sure our clothes were put on a table or chair out of reach of the insects. We put cheap talcum powder in little circles round all the chair and table legs. We had been told that no insect likes walking through powder, especially if it has a strong scent. It seemed to work well. One morning, Betty came into the kitchen holding up what remained of her knickers: a piece of elastic and a few shreds of fabric. In her broad Scots accent she cried, 'Will you look at this? Ma new panties, and the beasties ha' eaten them!' She had left them on a chair with no powder round it. I lost a pair of socks in the same way; we soon learned to make sure the powder was kept topped up but it made sweeping and dusting somewhat difficult.

We had a rota for the kitchen, bathroom and lounge cleaning – in theory at any rate. We took it in turns to do it for a week each, the only defaulter being Betty. She certainly did not like housework. The broom stayed firmly in the cupboard and dust drifted over everything. In all the corners cockroach shells could be spotted; usually in desperation, one of us would end up doing Betty's stint. Ron thought he could shame her into wielding the broom, so one day he made a pile of the cockroach shells in the middle of the floor. On the top he made a cross of matchsticks with a small notice reading 'R.I.P.' It made no difference – Betty joined in the laughter as much as the rest of us, and carried on exactly as before.

Another pest we had to contend with was ants. Not the ones that carved up the cockroach corpses but a small brown species called Argentine ants. They were reputed to be the only ones that could live in a fridge. They certainly lived in ours! Whatever food we had, whether it was in the cupboard or the fridge, always appeared covered in ants. At first, I used to throw the food away, until Mr Church said to me, 'You know, you are going to have to get used to this. These ants are quite clean little creatures – it's not like having flies on the food. Just bang the food on the table and they will run away.'

And so it proved: a hefty bang as the food was placed on the table and they would stream in all directions. Bread, cheese, meat and so on were easily dealt with; cake and sweet things were more difficult. The only thing I threw away once I got used to it was fig jam. This really defeated us – we couldn't see if we were spreading fig seeds or ants!

We saw Fred and Kate sometimes. Fred had found work on the same building site as Ron, but as he was unused to manual work he soon proved a danger to himself as well as to others. In England he had owned a men's hairdressing salon but was unable to obtain a Union ticket in Australia. There was a very strict Union rule: without a ticket it was impossible to obtain a job. Instead of weekly subscriptions, a whole year's payment had to be made before you could start work. In many ways this was unfair; work was hard to find and if anyone found a job in a different category, another year's Union money had to be paid. Hans and Dick had each paid a year in advance to the Carpenters and the Agricultural Union, then had to pay again to the General Labourer's Union. There was no escaping this practice. When they protested they were told no one would dare to employ them, they would be blacklisted. Without the appropriate ticket, no one worked.

Fred never managed to get his hairdressing ticket and he was finally asked to leave the building site after dropping a brick on the foreman's head! He eventually found a position in the big general hospital as a porter. To his amusement, one of his tasks was to wash and shave the male corpses and trim their beards and hair. As he said, 'It's a bit like my old job, I suppose; at least this time, none of my clients complain!'

Things were changing at Albion Road. Hans and Corrie were counting the days until they sailed; Dick was looking around for another job and the building project was nearing completion; we too were wondering what work would be available. Lisa continued to work at the mental hospital and was also nearing the time when she would be allowed to join her family in Sydney. One day, the famous Vienna Boys Choir came to Brisbane to give a concert. Lisa managed to purchase a ticket, and returned tear-stained but radiant. She had been invited to go back-stage and talk to some of the performers. She spoke German fluently as her home in Yugoslavia had been close to the Austrian border, so there was a shared patois, neither language pure but dialect understood by everyone. I think the opportunity to speak with people from her own area had proved almost too emotional. This little incident made me realise how alien these displaced people must feel, with nowhere really to call their own.

As the building site work neared its end, only weeks away, we started making plans. Dick and Betty decided to go back to farm work – it was the only kind of life they really enjoyed. They registered at several agencies and began to attend interviews. They were offered a position about sixty miles from Brisbane. Dick was to be a general farm hand but Betty was not required to work in the house. This suited her, as we knew she was not fond of housework! A house of sorts went with the job. We were all pleased for them and as Betty said, 'It will be too far from the racecourse for Dick to be tempted!'

Ron was looking, without success, for another job, so we thought we would try our luck in another state. I had corresponded occasionally with Jack and Janey Mount, who had been fellow passengers on the journey out. They lived a few miles from Perth so I wrote and asked what the prospects were in their area. Janey's reply was quite encouraging; the employment situation seemed more hopeful. Ron and I talked it over and decided to 'Go West'. Janey wrote and said she could find us a room to rent, so it was arranged.

We booked a passage on the train, a journey which would take six days and five nights and take us right across the continent, as far as if we were to have travelled from London to Turkey. There was a flurry of activity at Albion Road, most of us preparing to move on. Mr Church was going to have a fresh influx of residents – only Margie and Albert and old Mary would be left. Within a period of four weeks, four of his rooms would be empty.

There were goodbyes to say. We called on Fred and Kate; they were sorry to hear we were going so far away but we promised to keep in touch. We had a last meal with Phillip and Joy and arranged to meet them in Fremantle when they sailed round the coast on their way home later in the year.

Dick and Betty were the first to leave the house. They went the week before us, the taxi piled high with their belongings and the children waving excitedly from the back window as the rest of us stood outside to say goodbye. Hans, Corrie and Lisa would be leaving a few days after us, travelling to Sydney together, where Lisa would join her family, while Hans and Corrie embarked for the voyage to Holland.

The morning we left, we said goodbye to Mr Church before he went to his school, to Margie as she went off to the restaurant and to Old Mary as she tottered off with her shopping bag to the local store. We knocked on Albert's door. He was waiting as usual for his taxi to arrive to take him to the Day Centre. We tried to shake hands but he waved us away. 'Shan't say goodbye, mate,' he said, 'I'll be seeing you.' His behaviour was strange. We tried to explain that we probably would never see him again but he wouldn't listen. We escorted him to the front door and saw him off, looking old and tired as he hunched in the back seat.

'Poor old Albert,' Ron said, 'I believe he was really upset because we are leaving.'

I said, 'He is like most of us, I expect, hates goodbyes. He'll be all right when he gets to the centre and finds all his friends.'

Our taxi arrived a few moments later and we loaded our cases and our one big box. Hans, Corrie and Lisa stood on the verandah to wave us off and I felt quite sad. As the cab drew away, I looked back and the little group grew blurred through my tears. I thought of a proverb my old French teacher was fond of quoting. I can't remember the French, but it translated as 'To start out is to die a little', meaning that wherever you go, when you leave, a little piece of you always stays behind. In spite of all the drawbacks and inconveniences of life at Albion Road, we had shared such fun together and been like one family. 'Cheer up,' Ron said, 'You know the old saying, 'Go West, young man', well, here we go, we may be about to make our fortunes!'

The taxi turned the corner and Albion Road was lost to sight – again we were moving on.

Chapter 8

Going West

Brisbane Central Station was seething with activity: taxis coming and going, disgorging their passengers and luggage; vendors with their food trolleys dispensing coffee and sandwiches; and the general hustle and bustle that is common to rail termini anywhere in the world.

Most of the seats on the train were pre-booked by people travelling down to Sydney and we found our numbered seats easily. Needless to say, we were in a third class carriage, which meant we would have to sit up all night – no luxury bunk for us – but the train was clean and comfortable. We sat looking out of the window, watching the arrival of our fellow travellers. Suddenly Ron said, 'Look, isn't that the man from the Welfare Centre for the Blind, the man over there with the black briefcase? He's looking for someone, I think.' It was, indeed, the man from the Welfare Centre and we were the 'someone' he was looking for. He was peering in the windows as he walked down the train until he spotted us and hurried to our door.

'Oh, good, there you are. Mr Wood told me you were going to be on this train. Could you do me a favour?'

'Doing what?' Ron sounded puzzled.

'Well, it's a bit difficult. Albert Wood is also on this train, in a first class carriage. If you could keep an eye on him at odd times during the journey and see that he meets his family in Melbourne, it would be very helpful.'

I opened my mouth to ask some questions but at that moment the whistle blew and the train let out a great hiss of steam. There was a banging of doors and the usual garbled voice over the tannoy and, with a hasty 'It looks as if you are off,' the man thrust a piece of paper into Ron's hand. 'Here is his seat number, pop along and see him later, he'll explain everything.' He stepped back into the crowd waving from the platform and disappeared from sight.

The train moved smoothly off and we looked at each other. 'What on earth was all that about?' I asked.

'Goodness knows, we'll just have to wait and see. I'll give him time to settle down and then I'll pay him a visit,' Ron replied.

He spent more than an hour with Albert later in the morning while I read a story to Vivienne. When he returned he said, 'What a tale Albert had to tell!' and laughed. Apparently, Albert and Margie had lived in Melbourne with their respective spouses and families, and each day Albert had attended the Day Centre where Margie worked. They had been attracted to each other and a romance had blossomed, culminating in their flight to Brisbane, leaving their families behind. The saying that 'true love never runs smooth' certainly applied in this case.

The romance had soon lost its charm when they were forced, by financial circumstances, to live in the dreary room in Albion Road. We never knew how Albert's wife had found out his whereabouts – presumably through the Welfare Services. They had acted as mediators and finally arranged the reunion. I was annoyed. 'I think it has put us into a very awkward position. Albert has been jolly deceitful, he knew we were booked on this train, he must have told the Welfare people. It's all very well, leaving us to keep an eye on him during the journey, but expecting us to hand him over to his wife is the limit!'

Ron agreed, but there was nothing we could do about it. I couldn't help thinking of the unsuspecting Margie, who would return home from work that afternoon to find Albert gone, and would no doubt blame us for the whole affair. This, in fact, was exactly what happened. I received a letter from her a couple of weeks later at our new address in West Australia. It was vitriolic to say the least. She assumed we had arranged the reunion and encouraged Albert to deceive her. My reply, assuring her that we were innocent of any collusion and were dreadfully upset at being dragged in to act as 'minders' elicited a half-hearted apology, and I always felt that she probably had not believed us.

We had taken a packed lunch for the first day's journey, there being no dining facilities in the third class; as we ate our sandwiches, I thought of Albert, sitting down to a tasty lunch in the restaurant, being waited on by the smart young waiters, and hoped he was feeling too guilty to enjoy his meal!

It turned bitterly cold during the night. We hadn't thought to keep a couple of blankets with us; they were all packed away in the baggage van. Several times when we stopped at various stations, porters brought on board 'foot warmers'. These were large stone water bottles, filled with hot water, for us to rest our feet on. They reminded me of the old fashioned ones we used as children, very comforting.

We arrived in Sydney around seven thirty the next morning, disembarked, and sought out Albert. Leaving Ron to take care of him, I took Vivienne to the cloakrooms so we could have a proper wash. We had a long wait as the large rooms were crowded. 'Why are those girls wearing those funny hats, Mum?' Vivienne asked. It was true, every girl was wearing variations of turbans and fancy scarves. We soon saw why. Without exception, every single girl had enormous curlers in her hair. Out came the curlers, then make-up cases were produced, on went the powder, lipstick, mascara and eye shadow, hair was brushed and back-combed and, amid much giggling and chattering, a hundred Sydney misses were ready to go to work. It was obviously the usual morning routine. I suppose it gave the participants an extra half-hour in bed!

We had several hours to explore part of Sydney before our next train was due to leave, but with Albert in tow, we were unable to move very far, though we were able to enjoy the fresh air and a leisurely meal at lunch time before returning to the station for the second stage of our long journey. The train which was to carry us to Melbourne was more luxurious than the one from Brisbane, with reclining seats and spacious compartments, very much like the interior of an aircraft. I looked forward to a comfortable night – in vain! On board was a team of young hockey players, returning West after a match in Sydney: a successful outcome, I imagine, as they were full of high spirits, both bottled and otherwise! Boys will be boys, as they say, and these were no exception; they spent the whole night playing pranks on each other.

The seats immediately in front of us were occupied by a young Italian couple with two small babies. One was about a year old and the other new-born, not more than a few weeks. Judging from the labels on their luggage, they had only just arrived in the country and certainly they spoke no English. The mother evidently had no food with her, there were no facilities on board for making baby food and the two infants wailed continuously. I wondered if the new child had actually been born on board ship; all immigrants arrived by ship at that time, air passages being too expensive. A large dummy was popped in first one open mouth and then the other. The father finally gave up trying to sleep and presumably found a seat in another carriage. He certainly didn't reappear until the journey was almost over. It was a very long and noisy night!

We changed trains early in the morning for the last leg to Melbourne. The train for the actual run into the city was called *The Spirit of Progress*; it was the last word in luxury and quite a talking point among the passengers. I was sorry we were not going to travel the rest of the way on it. We arrived at mid-morning and sought Albert out. The big moment had arrived! We stood on the platform, surrounded by his and our cases, and looked at the crowds greeting their friends and relatives.

Albert looked ill at ease, as well he might! We had no idea what his wife looked like and he, being blind, could not search for her himself, so there we stood. As the crowd thinned a small, anxious-looking woman, accompanied by a much younger woman, came toward us. So this was the real Mrs Wood! As tiny as Margie had been large, pale and quietly spoken, she took Albert diffidently by the arm. We felt so embarrassed as they greeted each other, and followed them out to the waiting room, between us carrying the various pieces of baggage. We heard her say, 'Who are these people, Albert?'

He muttered, 'Just some people I met on the train, they have kindly kept an eye on me.'

She thanked us for our help, we all shook hands and wished him well, and left him with his wife and the younger woman, whom we assumed was his daughter, although she hadn't spoken a word. We wondered what sort of a reunion it would turn out to be; needless to say, we never heard of Albert again.

The most interesting part of the journey was the crossing of the Nullabor Plain. We had spent a day in Adelaide after an uneventful trip from Melbourne to the capital of South Australia. This time there were no bush fires raging, as there had been during our voyage out, so we explored parts of the city with pleasure. A dirty train to Port Pirie Junction somewhat dampened my spirits. The regular travellers knew how to cope; they all carried dusters and cleaned the seats before they sat down!

An elderly Italian couple sat opposite us, and the lady, like most Italians, adored children. She paid a great deal of attention to Vivienne, patting her head and talking to her in Italian. I said to her husband, 'Have you only come to Australia recently, or are you visiting your relations?'

He replied, 'Oh no, we have been here almost fifty years, but mamma, she speaka no English!'

We were amazed, but later found this to be quite common. The mothers of many European families spend most of their time indoors, mixing only with their families, and so never feel the need to learn any language other than their native one.

Covered in dust and with filthy hands, we left the train and joined the Trans-Continental Express in the late afternoon. The Express was air-conditioned; each cabin had a wash basin and a radio; at the ends of each corridor were shower rooms and toilets – luxury indeed. We were able to clean ourselves before the evening meal.

All the seats were reserved, the only snag being that men and women were separated. Vivienne and I were sharing with two retired school teachers from New Zealand. As this part of the journey took twenty-four hours, we heard all about their long-awaited retirement holiday. They were pleasant company and devoted to each other. At bedtime, the bunks were pulled down and linen provided by the smart attendants. I was in a top bunk with Vivienne underneath, the two ladies opposite. We had settled down to sleep when suddenly one of the ladies said, 'Oh dear, Elsie, I haven't kissed you goodnight.' So on went the lights, she got out of her bunk with great difficulty, unhooked the ladder, climbed to the top bunk with much puffing and grunting, kissed her friend and climbed down again. I hoped it was worth the bother!

Ron wasn't so fortunate with his fellow travellers. He shared with an English sailor, a Bulgarian and an Australian. They had an inexhaustible supply of whisky, which they consumed by the tumblerful all night long. Ron, being no drinker, declined to join them, and as the night wore on, I gather it became somewhat lively! No one went to sleep and I suspect that the folk in the adjoining cabin didn't sleep much either.

After our breakfast in the dining car, we went to the observation coach, a large compartment at the rear of the train. It had windows all round and plenty of space for the children to move about.

The Nullabor Plain is a vast desert, a thousand miles across, we were told. The train made only brief halts, to fill the water tanks; no one got on or off. Every hundred miles or so were small settlements, just a few timber or asbestos shacks, where the men who maintained the permanent way lived. Some of them had their families with them; a few had even made an effort to create little gardens out of that barren land. Nearly all the residents were Italian or East Europeans. The twice-weekly arrival of the train was a great event, for whenever we stopped, the people clustered around the doors, asking for sweets or fruit. If someone passed out a magazine or a newspaper, the adults were delighted. I could not imagine how anyone could tolerate such isolation; little did I realise that within a year, I, too, would be living in similar circumstances.

There was very little wild life to be seen, a few kangaroo or emu, salt bush or scraggy gum trees the only foliage. Sometimes a small group of aboriginals with some lean cattle could be spotted as we flashed by. Twenty-four hours passed so quickly; I felt we should never experience such a journey again. We changed trains at Kalgoorlie, which had once been a thriving gold-mining town. Many of the mines were now disused, the seams having petered out. One of the legacies of those wild days remained in the fact that the public houses stayed open day and night. This had been so that the miners could always slake their thirst whenever they came from their shifts underground.

We boarded the Westland Express in the evening for the last leg, to Perth, our destination. The Westland was nothing like the Trans-Continental! In fact, it was just like a train out of a Western film, even down to the little caboose at the rear. A canvas bag hung there: anyone wanting a drink of water had to go outside and use the tin mug provided. I found myself watching out for Wyatt Earp!

We slept well, although not in such comfort as the previous night, but after six days on the move, I think we could have slept anywhere! It had been a wonderful trip, the crossing of the entire continent, but we were relieved to see the skyline of Perth ahead and to know we had reached journey's end. We gathered our belongings together, watching, as the train slowed down, to see if we could spot Janey, who was coming to meet us. We had come West, like the old pioneers, but not, I hoped, to suffer the same conditions! Another new beginning lay ahead.

Chapter 9

Settling In

Janey was waiting for us on the platform and standing with her was a tall dark man, to whom she introduced us. This was Jonnie Casey, her next-door neighbour. He was half aboriginal, an immensely strong man who looked strangely ill at ease in his dark suit. Janey explained that Jack was unable to take time off from his work to be with her, so Jonnie had volunteered to come and help with the luggage. We boarded a small local train to complete the journey – the area where we were to live was about ten miles distant.

Jack and Janey had purchased a plot of land from Jonnie on which they had built a bungalow. Jonnie, although unable to read or write, certainly knew how to make money! He owned several plots of land at Tinton and also apparently acted as a local moneylender, his wife, Maud, doing the book-keeping. Our new landlady was called Mrs Shale, and Janey and Jonnie took us to her house, only a few hundred yards from the railway halt, made the introductions and left us to settle in.

The house was the usual asbestos-covered iron-roofed dwelling. built on legs with zinc caps to prevent termites and other insects from invading the inside. It had only three rooms, two bedrooms at the front and a living room at the rear. A narrow verandah opened into a tiny bathroom, containing an old porcelain bath, brown-stained, as the water was always the colour of beer. An enamel bowl stood on a stool to act as a wash basin. A hut, some way distant, across the grass, was the toilet.

The plot itself was large and part of it was a makeshift sawmill, housed in a few tin huts. Mrs Shale's son, Will, cut and sold wood and made his home in a Humpy, close by his wood piles. The Humpy held a camp bed, a cupboard and a chair, the rest of the room being taken up with piles and piles of books, mostly paper-back thrillers. They leaned drunkenly in all directions, yellowed with age and nibbled by mice. There was no window so the door invariably stood open, to lend a little light to the dark interior. A stone trough in a lean-to served as a bathroom and a canvas bag held his washing water. He ate his meals with his mother but his visits were brief, for only as long as it took him to demolish the food.

Mrs Shale was a striking-looking woman in her seventies, tall and majestic, with deep-set eyes, a hooked nose and white hair plaited round her head. Although born in Australia, she had no accent but spoke in a deep cultured voice. She was widely travelled and well educated, as, we found later, were her sons and daughter.

When we had unpacked our cases in the small bedroom we were to rent, we went into the living room where tea had been prepared. The furniture was very basic: a square deal table, six Windsor chairs, a cupboard, a refrigerator and a wood stove for cooking and heating. Mrs Shale produced a piece of chalk and drew a line across the middle of the table.

'Today you will eat with me,' she said firmly, 'Tomorrow that will be your end of the table, where you will always have your meals, providing your own food, of course. I expect you to find a permanent home of your own as soon as possible, naturally.'

We felt like school children. She repeated the chalk mark in the fridge: we were to have two shelves. At least we knew where we stood. We retired to our room soon after the meal with mixed feelings as to our future in the West.

Next morning we were up early as Ron wanted to go into Perth to register for a job – we didn't want a repetition of our experiences in Brisbane. There was no sound from the other bedroom, so we crept about, stoked the fire as quietly as we could to boil a kettle, helped ourselves to cereal and started our meal. We spoke in whispers for fear of waking Mrs Shale but, although we had not heard her moving, the door to her room opened suddenly and she appeared. She was wearing a dressing gown, her white hair flowed down her back and she reminded me of an Indian Chief, minus the feathered head-dress. It was not that which left me with with a spoonful of cornflakes poised half-way to my mouth, but the object she held in front of her. In her right hand, held at length, was an enormous chamber pot, full to the brim!

'Good morning,' she snapped, marched purposefully to the door, opened it, and flung the contents of the pot as far across the rough grass as she could. The trough near the door which was used for laundry had a tap on a stand pipe; she rinsed the pot under this and stepped back inside. My face must have registered my surprise – I have never been able to conceal my feelings! She stared at me for a few seconds, then said, 'You can take that look off your face, young lady. If you think five people can use that lavatory for everything, you can think again!'

She pointed across the grass to the little hut, emphasising her words with a stabbing finger. 'That is for BIG JOBS ONLY. The Road Board people come when they think they will, not every week. I will give you a bucket to keep in your room. You will have to do the same as Will and I do, like it or not. Understand? BIG JOBS ONLY!'

She went back into her room and closed the door. Ron and I looked at each other and collapsed into helpless laughter. I moaned, 'If my mother could see me now!'

As the weeks passed, we realised the old lady was absolutely right: the Road Board men came to empty the pan at irregular intervals, sometimes after a week, or it could be more than a fortnight. Either way, it didn't make a lot of difference – the pan would be a heaving mass of maggots. No one used it unless it was necessary. Our bucket had to be emptied in the mornings in the same way hers was, but I could never bring myself to carry it through the living room. I used to open our bedroom window and throw the contents across the grass as far as possible, the result being that the grass round our side of the house turned a deeper shade of yellow by the day!

The night cart, as it was called, was manned by men called 'offsiders'. Their jobs were always being advertised, which was not surprising! As in the outskirts of Brisbane, they came in the daytime, in a large two-tiered truck, the top tier holding the empty cans with the full ones placed at the bottom. We were not allowed to use any kind of disinfectant or antiseptic – something to do with destroying the natural bacteria. I thought the idea of the boxes of sawdust that were used in Brisbane was much more hygienic. The arrival of the night cart was always heralded by a cloud of flies. If you didn't happen to see it coming, it could also be very embarrassing! The toilet huts were built with a hinged flap at the back, which the 'offsiders' would lift to remove the full pan. I was visiting a friend one day and went out to use her toilet. Seated there, to my horror, the flap in the back was suddenly raised and a large hairy arm came in to take the pan! I flew off the seat, cowered against the wall and hoped I couldn't be seen, while the arm came in again with the clean pan. The flap closed and I sat down again, almost hysterical with a fit of giggling. I never got caught again! I think my life in Australia was haunted by 'loo' experiences.

Ron found a job with a roofing firm, a trade he had learnt as a youngster. He enjoyed it but it meant he was away quite a lot, travelling to country districts mostly, where the wealthier farmers could afford to have tiled roofs. Vivienne and I made a few friends locally, we visited Janey and Jack often and their ten year old daughter; we also grew friendly with a couple who kept a small grocery store. May was English and Alan, her husband, Scottish. We had a lot in common and their youngest child was the same age as Vivienne, so she had someone to play with. Another family with three children lived near us: the father was of German parentage and the mother was a first generation Australian, and these few families became our closest companions.

We spent as much time as possible away from our room at Mrs Shale's. I felt that a small child playing around the plot would worry her, and the open-fronted sawmill with its great circular saws was an ever-present danger. Mrs Shale herself was an interesting character. She had been married at the turn of the century and, with her husband, had done the 'Grand Tour of Europe' as they used to call it, as a honeymoon trip. They had had a large sheep station in the Murchison district, also a gold mine. She had borne three sons and a daughter but had been deeply unhappy in her marriage. Whenever she mentioned her husband, which was seldom, it was with such bitterness, as if she had really hated him. When the children had grown up, she left him, walking away without a penny. She had come down to Perth and found a job, and eventually trained as a hairdresser. For some years she owned and worked in her own salon; in fact from time to time she still cut and permed a neighbour's hair.

When she was of retirement age she sold the business and bought the small house where she still lived. The gold mine had ceased to be a profitable one and her sons had gone their separate ways, Will, having been recently divorced, coming to live with his mother. The arrangement had been unsuccessful from the start, so Will had erected his Humpy, built his sawmill and came to the house as little as possible. The one daughter of Mrs Shale's marriage stayed with her father on the sheep station. On his death, she had inherited everything and her relationship with her mother was distant. She wrote occasionally but only visited once a year, not to stay. In spite of her forceful manner I always felt Mrs Shale was probably a very lonely old lady.

Bearing in mind the fact that were were to find a permanent home as quickly as we could, we started to find out the prices and location of plots of land. Most of the plots were a third of an acre and they were easy to find. Although we did not particularly want to stay in Tinton, it seemed to be the most sensible thing to do. Ron had been offered a job at the mill where

Jonnie was the foreman. The money was slightly better than the roofing firm and it would mean he would be home all the time, so he duly started to learn to be a miller. The hours were long: two shifts, seven a.m. to three p.m. and three to eleven p.m. There were no breaks at all as the machines must never be allowed to stop, only at night for the necessary maintenance. The product was mainly oats and it was hard, noisy and extremely dusty work, no doubt the reason all people called Miller are nicknamed Dusty!

Ron enjoyed the work and found Jonnie a real character to work for. After we had looked at a number of plots, Jonnie asked us if we would like the last one of his, which abutted his own garden; we thought it over and decided to accept the offer. His wife Maud agreed that we could use their toilet, and once a week do some cooking on her stove. We applied for permission to put a small caravan on the site while we were actually building a house, and this was granted. Legal formalities were much more relaxed than in England and in a few weeks we had obtained permission for the caravan and completed the sale of the plot. We were to pay Jonnie a sum of money each week, plus, of course, the usual interest, until the land was ours. We told Mrs Shale we were leaving and in spite of her brusque manner towards us, I think she was sorry to see us go. We visited her often and kept her up-to-date with all our doings.

We bought a book of bungalow designs and spent hours poring over the ones we liked, and working out a budget. In the end we found they were all beyond our price; we could not have borrowed the sum of money required, not on Ron's wages anyway. Finally, we compromised – we would do the same as the rest of them – build half a house! We chose an L--shaped plan, one wing containing a lounge, a kitchen and the compulsory (at that time) laundry room. The other wing would have three bedrooms and the bathroom, when we could afford it! After all, when in Rome, etc.

Our tiny touring caravan was towed to the plot and we moved in. We had hired the van for an initial period of ten weeks with an option to extend the period if necessary. Ron would have quite a lot of free time; on his early shift he could work in the afternoons and evenings, and the late shifts would give him free mornings. We had been assured by all the near neighbours that when he actually started, there would be plenty of willing helpers. This would be a great help as Ron's woodwork experience consisted of the construction of a rough hen house when he was about twelve years old!

He drew up the required three copies of the house design on graph paper, worked out all the specifications down to the last nail, and submitted them to the local council. It took longer to get them dealt with than it had to purchase the land, but the day of acceptance came and we ordered the timbers to lay the floor joists. Somehow, all the people who had been so keen to lend a hand found there was something of great importance they had to do instead. Like most of our schemes, it looked as if this one would also go 'agley' and whatever problems would lie ahead in the building of a house, we would have to sort them out ourselves.

We put the profiles into the sandy soil to show the shape of our house-to-be and felt quite excited as we stood and imagined the end result. The timbers arrived and were stacked neatly in piles, the boxes of nails were ready for rubbing with hard soap to make them easier to hammer into the Jarrah, which is an exceedingly hard wood; our half-a-house was under way!

Chapter 10

Half a House

During the building of our half-a-house, the weather was extremely hot. It was early autumn (although of course Australian seasons are not a bit like ours) but the temperatures were in the high eighties. The small caravan was unbearable: we were unable to stay in it during the day. Once breakfast was over, I would go out onto our plot and sit under the paper bark tree, seeking what shade there was. Whenever Ron was working on the house, I was available to help in any way I could, mainly pushing the nails in and out of the hard soap or helping to hold the wooden frames while Ron nailed them into place. We had to hire a carpenter to pitch the roof as it needed some professional skill, and it certainly needed two pairs of strong arms to lift the timbers. The man we hired was an Englishman who rejoiced in the name of Peter Piper. I wanted to ask him if he had ever 'picked a peck of pickled pepper' but thought he would have heard that old joke too many times before. Although he lived quite near, we never saw his wife; she had developed a heart condition two or three years before and was virtually housebound. In the hot weather she stayed indoors, lying down, with a fan continually creating a little breeze. What a different way of life from the one they had led in England, where she had run a small business and been surrounded by family and friends.

In spite of the heat and cramped conditions in the van, I managed to cook some satisfying meals. We only had a primus stove, a lethal object with a will of its own. When I was a child we had used them frequently in the country but I had never actually lit one. The instructions were easy to follow: 'Pour a little methylated spirit into the small saucer beneath the main burner. Light the spirit, wait a few seconds until most of it has evaporated, them pump briskly (figure four), apply a lighted match to the main burner which should be burning evenly within thirty seconds. The flame may then be adjusted (figure six) and cooking commence.'

Sounded straightforward enough; in practice it wasn't that easy. Nine times out of ten the flames shot up to the ceiling of the van and I invariably panicked and rushed outside, slamming the door behind me. I would wait until the flames died down before venturing inside and placing the saucepan over the burner. Once the stove was well alight, it cooked very well. I had an enormous stewpan which I would balance on the top, propped up by three sticks, a highly dangerous performance. In this way I could roast a whole dinner: a piece of beef surrounded by carrots, parsnips and potatoes, with a pudding in a basin on the top! Necessity certainly is the mother of invention as well as the father!

Once a week I paid Maud a few shillings to use her wood stove to do some baking and to wash our bed linen in her copper. She also allowed us to use her shower once a week and, as the water was always luke warm, it was at no cost to her. Living in the van has put Ron off caravan holidays for life! When he was on the early shift, he had his breakfast at six a.m. and as the table we ate at formed part of the bed, he had to eat standing up. Vivienne and I stayed in bed until later as there was so little room, so Ron would balance his plate on the small draining board and had to keep his head bent because of the low-pitched ceiling. He said he knew just how a horse must feel!

We had an ice box in one corner which contained a large block of ice. This was delivered three times a week and it certainly helped to keep the food cool, but as the daily temperatures rose higher, the block would melt away by lunchtime, the water trickling away through the drainage hole into the parched ground under the van. Although the heat in the day was so hard to bear, at night it grew very cold – the temperature could drop by as much as thirty degrees, which made it seem almost winter-like. The plywood walls were so thin that we shivered under our blankets; when the wind blew, it rocked the van to and fro so violently that we frequently ended up on the floor. Ron made a rope barrier which he fixed to the side of the upper bunk so that Vivienne wouldn't have a long drop if she should fall. When I see some of the lovely mobile homes today, I compare them with our rickety little van!

The plot of land we had purchased was situated on a swamp and as soon as it was dusk the dykes became alive with frogs. The noise was unbelievable. The first time we heard it we couldn't think what it was. First there was a loud 'Wheeee, wheeee' followed by a deep 'Plonk, plonk', and all around other weird noises grew, exactly as if a symphony orchestra was tuning up. We found, on enquiring from Maud next day, that these were indeed called the 'Orchestra' frogs. There were Banjo frogs, Violin frogs and so on because of their musical croaks, each one performing his own little tune. As the night wore on the noise would die away to be replaced with a variety of other strange sounds, from birds and insects unfamiliar to us.

One day Ron came home from work carrying two tiny pigeons, only a few days old. They had fallen from their nests high in the mill roof and been pounced on by the stray cats, to be snatched away in the nick of time. They had no feathers and their eyes were still closed and they were the ugliest creatures I had ever seen. Their beaks were enormous, opening and shutting continually and giving forth a feeble squeak.

'What on earth are you going to do with them?' I asked.

'Try and rear them of course, I just couldn't let them be killed,' he replied.

So we found a cardboard box, filled it with torn-up paper and it became their nest. Ron used to bring corn and maize from the mill, chew it up and feed it to the birds in exactly the same way as their mothers would have done. In fact, they regarded him as their mother and as soon as they were able to scramble in and out of their box, they would nestle under his arms, making little cooing noises and he would coo back at them. We called them Bluey and Stripey and they grew into handsome birds. It took some time to teach them to fly – we used to throw them to each other as if they were soft balls until they instinctively flapped their wings. In all the snapshots taken at that time they can been seen perched on Ron's shoulder or sitting on the end of the saw as he cut the timbers. The day the van was towed away and the house was ready to move into they were distressed, hovering around, not knowing where to settle. We had grown so fond of them and hoped they would settle with us in the house. We tried to encourage them to come indoors, with no success – they would perch on the roof but that was all. Eventually they flew off together. We hoped they were a 'pigeon pair' and would perhaps mate one day.

We were aiming to have the house ready for occupation by Christmas Day – the van rental was quite high so we wanted to dispense with it as soon as possible. The day came when the roof was pitched, the asbestos sheets were nailed to timber studs and we were able to choose our roof tiles. We had decided to have a 'proper' roof instead of the usual corrugated iron and found there was a quarry some miles away where tiles were manufactured. To save money, Ron was going to do the tiling himself and we found we could purchase the tiles on a cash and carry basis. Will Shale agreed to provide the transport with himself as the driver, and Ron of course doing the choosing of colour and size. On the morning we had arranged to hire Will, Ron had his shift changed to the early one, owing to some trouble with staff at the mill, so I was delegated to go with Will. Armed with the cheque book I waited with Vivienne for Will to arrive. It was a scorcher of a day, over a hundred degrees, and when we climbed into the truck it felt like the inside of an oven. I was wearing a pink linen dress and a pair of high-heeled white sandals. With hindsight, I should have chosen a pair of overalls!

By the time we reached the quarry and I had been into the office to choose the colour we wanted, sign the necessary forms and pay, it was around noon. The office manager pointed out the direction of the working area, deep in the quarry, where the tiles would be loaded and Will drove the truck down. It was evidently the start of the lunch break as all the men, clad only in bush hats, brief shorts and heavy boots, were sitting about smoking, drinking cans of beer and eating sandwiches. Clutching my invoice, I dismounted and approached the man I assumed to be the foreman, as he was the only one dressed in shirt and trousers.

'May we have these tiles please?' I held out my paper. He glanced at it, looked down at me and drawled, 'Yeah, help yourself.' He turned his back on me and walked away. I ran after him.

'I want four and a half thousand.'

'Yeah, so I see, well there they are. Like I said, help yourself.' He jerked a thumb at the tall stacks. 'You load your own, we only load trade orders.' He walked back to his beer and lunch box.

I stood unbelieving, surely they didn't expect me to load them? They did! All those husky men sitting around grinning; not one of them moved. I laid my white handbag in the cab, told Vivienne not to move and went to the rear of the truck and let down the heavy flap. I started to load the tiles. Will stayed in the driving seat, looking somewhat embarrassed, but made no effort to climb out. I suppose he thought that we had hired his truck and his services as a driver but not as a navvy! I started lifting five tiles at a time, they were very heavy and almost too hot to handle; within a short time I could only manage three. Down in that sheltered spot the temperature must have been all of 115°F. My clothes were sticking to my back, perspiration dripped off my forehead and into my eyes and my lovely pink dress was already filthy. Breathless and furious, I turned to the men and shouted, 'If any one of you was a gentleman, at least you would lend me a hat.' The foreman took off his greasy bush hat and whistled it across to me as if it were a frisbee. I thanked him and crammed it down on my head.

I could hear the men chuckling and making remarks such as "Typical

Pommie Sheelagh', and so on but I was determined not to let them see me give in. Gradually, the piles in the truck grew but clambering up and down with each armful was exhausting work and I was getting slower each minute. At last, Will moved. I think he felt shamed into helping me. He tied four knots in his grubby handkerchief, placed it on his bald head, and descended from his cab. It felt as if there were forty thousand tiles, not four, by the time we had finished the loading and a cheer went up from the work force as we drove away. I gave a wave and a grin, although I felt like making a very different gesture! My sandals were torn to ribbons, my dress likewise, fit only for the rag bag, and my hands were bleeding from the rough tiles.

When I had calmed down a little I suggested to Will that he stopped at the nearest public house as I felt we needed a drink. He agreed and presently drew up in the car park of a large pub. I walked into the bar and asked for a pint of beer for Will and lemonade for Vivienne and myself. Will, the colour of a boiled beetroot and puffing like a steam engine, came up behind me. Before he could say anything, the publican hissed, 'Get that kid out of here. NOW.' I should have thought; nice women did not go into Australian pubs. Vivienne and I had to go outside and sit on the grass verge with our drinks.

On our arrival back at the van I made some sandwiches and a pot of tea and changed into jeans and a pair of heavy shoes before we tackled the unloading of those endless tiles. We had just finished when Ron arrived home from work. He was amazed when I told him my tale; we have laughed about it many times since then but I think that was the hardest and hottest job of my life! Will wrote out his account, ten shillings an hour, four hours and eleven minutes, plus extra because he had actually done some labour as well! I don't think he had worked so hard for years.

Ron tiled the roof during the next few days, finishing it one night by the light of the full moon! We were running out of time. He hired some floor cramps to lay the floorboards with and together we glazed the windows. We hired a neighbour to help put up the guttering as it was too heavy for me and by the time the front door was hung it looked quite a professional job. The van was due to be collected in a few days, so I went into Perth to buy the basic items of furniture we could afford to set up home with. At an army surplus stores I purchased a camp bed for Vivienne and a mattress for ourselves, a folding picnic table and four small chairs. I managed to find a second hand cooker but as the electricity wasn't going to be connected until after Christmas, we would have to use the primus stove or cook outside, gypsy fashion, for a week or two. We certainly wouldn't find the living room cramped: our mattress would be rolled up during the day. Our clothes would have to stay in the trunk and our food in boxes as we had no money for cupboards. It wasn't going to be a palace but it would be our first real home since we had left England.

Chapter 11

Life at Number Seven

Our house was allocated number seven; we didn't know why, as it was the only dwelling on that side of the short dirt road. December 22nd arrived and we moved in with our few belongings. There were no inner walls, just the timber frames, as we had used all our money, so all the finishing touches would have to be met from the weekly wages. In the small room which would eventually be the laundry room, only half the floor was boarded, which, to begin with, was fortunate. We had no money to build even a primitive toilet and a bathroom was to be added when the second half of the house was built, so we decided the open area of the floor could be used for the disposal of our bodily waste! We used a bucket, set in the corner, and simply emptied the contents under the floorboards. Definitely not to be recommended in temperatures of over 100 degrees!

As soon as we were able to purchase three more sheets of asbestos, Ron dug a large pit at the bottom of our plot and constructed a rough hut to serve as a toilet. There was no roof or door but two sacks were acquired from the mill, cut in halves and a curtain made. Not very successful as the sacks were thin and, sitting on the seat, you could wave to people going up the road! The sun beat down mercilessly through the open roof onto our heads, so our visits were, of necessity, brief. Very much the hot seat!

Joy and Phillip were landing at Fremantle in the early morning of the 22nd, so later they arrived to see us. There wasn't much comfort to offer them, but Phillip helped Ron to complete several jobs outside the house while Joy and I cooked a meal on a camp fire. We spent the next two days together, although they went back to the ship to sleep. How I envied them their coming trip, even knowing what a poor sailor I was. They were sailing on Christmas Eve and we went by bus down to the docks to say 'Goodbye'. The weather was so hot that it was almost impossible to stand on the quayside; the customs sheds and warehouses were made of corrugated iron and reflected the midday heat. We were able to go on board and see their cabin and stay about half an hour before the 'All visitors ashore' was piped.

There was a long wait after the gang planks were drawn up before the ship began to move. Crowds lined the quay, all straining to see their friends and relatives on deck; the band played 'Now is the hour' and 'Anchors aweigh' as the ship drew slowly out to sea. The passengers threw brightly coloured paper streamers to be caught by those on shore and we caught some thrown by Joy and Phillip. We watched as they grew taut and stretched as the distance between us widened. Gradually the paper snapped and hundreds of streamers floated gently into the water like fragments of a broken rainbow. The sound of the music grew fainter and the faces became a blur; many people were in tears as they watched their loved ones sail away. The ship turned, the hooters blew and the vessel steamed away on the long journey.

We returned to our house, very subdued. A parcel awaited us from home and there were several cards and letters, but it didn't feel a bit like Christmas. We exchanged small gifts next morning and opened our presents from home; Ron turned the portable radio on and the voice of Bing Crosby filled the room singing 'Silent Night'. I burst into tears. 'Switch it off, I can't stand it,' I cried. The thought of those at home, playing games round the fire, roasting chestnuts, eating turkey and mince pies, the tree with all the lights and small gifts was just too much to bear. We had no special dinner, cold corned beef and tomatoes was all that our budget allowed. I couldn't wait for the day to end.

With the new year, life settled into some sort of routine. Ron continued working at the mill and Vivienne and I led a very quiet life. Saturday nights were the highlight of the week, when there was always a picture show in the village hall. The screen was enormous and the sound track set at one pitch, loud, and there seemed no way of reducing the volume. We always went, in self-defence really. It was better to be there and follow the story than to sit indoors hearing every word of the dialogue without knowing the story! We sat on hard wooden chairs while hoards of small children ran up and down the aisles, clad in their pyjamas, eating all manner of sticky sweets, crisps and fruit, so it was hard to concentrate on the plot. It wasn't exactly the 'Odeon' but it was a break in routine.

One night as we returned from the show, I entered our house first, put out my hand to switch on the light and encountered something warm and soft. The switch was above the unseen object and when light flooded the room I saw, with horror, the biggest spider I have ever seen. It was the size of a saucer, had enormous hairy legs, and took off down the wall and across the floor at quite a pace. My shrieks brought Ron, who took off his shoe and attacked it. No success – it scuttled towards the stove. He grabbed a garden trowel which was in the corner and hit it again. Appalled, I watched as half of it fell away and died, while the other half ran behind the stove where we couldn't get at it. As we lay on our mattress on the floor that night, I couldn't sleep – I kept thinking that the other half of the creature would come back and walk over me! I know the old saying, 'If you want to live and thrive, let a spider run alive', but when you don't know which are poisonous, it doesn't do to take chances.

Spiders were quite a problem in West Australia; in Queensland it had been the cockroaches as well as spiders – here it was a number of different species. Funnel web and trap-door spiders were highly dangerous. We rarely saw these, but the little red-backs were a menace. They made their homes in dark places – coat sleeves, shoes and, the most popular, under toilet seats. Here they would spin a single web, sit in the middle and wait for the unsuspecting bottom to descend! They were small, about the size of a finger nail, with a hard shell of bright red, similar to a ladybird. Although their bite was not fatal, it could result in partial paralysis or a weak heart, so we were careful to look inside our sleeves and shoes before putting them on and we always took a torch to shine down our pit before we used our toilet. Luckily, we were never bitten but we knew several people who had been.

As soon as it was dusk each day a strong breeze blew up, known as the Fremantle Doctor. This brought with it myriads of unknown insects, which crawled up and down our walls at will; as there were no inside wall panels, they had free access with open spaces top and bottom. During January we had three days and nights of torrential rain, which was most unusual, the rainy season being in June and July. We lay on our mattress and watched the water pour down the inside of our walls in a cascade, washing hundreds of insects down, only to see a fresh contingent struggling up the walls from under the house. I wish we had possessed a camera of the instant variety such as is on the market today; we could have taken a few prizewinning pictures. One result of the out-of-season rain was the crop of ready-cooked vegetables which were dug from the gardens. The humid conditions and warm rain had actually steamed the vegetables in the ground. I sent the cuttings from the local papers home as I felt no one would believe it unless they saw it in print.

We became good friends with a young couple from Birmingham, Derek and Maureen Greenfield, who lived a few miles up the railway line from us, and Derek worked with Ron at the mill. They had bought a plot of land on which there was already a garage. Like so many others, they hoped to save enough money to build a house in time. Their early days in Australia had been difficult: Maureen had been pregnant when they travelled out and their first home with distant relatives had proved unfriendly. In desperation they had rushed into buying the first plot they could afford. Our home was pretty basic but theirs was even worse. The baby was about a year old when we met them and, apart from an ancient push-chair, Maureen had no baby equipment at all. The garage contained a stone trough to serve as bath, kitchen sink and laundry, a mattress for them all to sleep on and a sewing machine in a lovely cabinet brought from home and much treasured.

We used to visit them one week and share a meal and the next week they would visit us. At their home we all sat round on the mattress to eat our meal, while the baby slept soundly at one end. Maureen had an old wood stove on which she cooked some delicious meals. It never seemed strange to us, sitting on the hard mattress, balancing our plates on our laps; we just accepted the fact that our lives out there in no way resembled the life we had left in England. One night when they had been to visit us and were walking up the dusty track towards their home, Maureen had a horrible experience. They were just passing the one street light when something detached itself from the lamp post and landed on Maureen's foot. It was a huge black spider which clung to her toe. She was wearing open-toed sandals so had no protection. Derek admitted that he had been really scared himself. He took off his shoe and beat it but it would not let go. He couldn't prise it loose until he had killed it, by which time, Maureen was almost fainting. She had been badly bitten and Derek had a job to half carry her home while dragging the pushchair as well.

Maureen was vomiting by now and semi-conscious, so Derek called his only near neighbour. While Derek made hot coffee the neighbour ran to the nearest phone but could not get a doctor to call. All night long, they walked Maureen up and down, plying her with black coffee at intervals – anything to keep her awake and on the move. By morning, she was feeling better but very tired and weak. As no one they knew had a car, she went by train to the nearest doctor. To this day she does not know what sort of a spider it was or what form of poisoning she had suffered from. Luckily, there were no lasting effects but, like me, she still has this terror of spiders. When she found she was pregnant with their second child she sold her precious sewing machine to pay part of the fare home, leaving Derek to follow when he had saved the money.

We exchanged letters quite often and I remember she wrote to me, saying, 'How wonderful it is to be home, even if it means staying with my mother until Derek returns. The first time I was able to flush a toilet, I shouted "Hurrah", and again when I saw a dustman collecting rubbish from outside the gate, and when the bus conductor called me "Love", then I knew I was really home.' We still meet a couple of times a year and it's always a case of 'Do you remember' and the spider stories are shuddered over again.

Our other good friends were May and Alan Brown. They had spent most of their married life in Persia, as it was then called; Alan had been an engineer in the oil fields. When the political situation had become so difficult that it was impossible for them to stay, they had come to Australia, hoping that Alan would find a situation in the Kwinana Oilfields which were just coming into production near Fremantle. The usual Union ticket procedure had prevented this so they had purchased the grocery store in Tinton, hoping that he would be able to return to his own profession in due course. I don't think he was very happy as a grocer but with so little work being available, he hadn't much choice.

The most interesting character around was Jonnie Casey. Although his origins were uncertain, his father had probably been a white farmer; it had been the accepted thing for a farmer to take a native wife as white women were few and far between in the outback, particularly in the early days of the century. The first things Jonnie could recall were living with his mother, who was an aboriginal girl, and the man who was then his mother's partner. Casey was the name by which Jonnie was known but he had no idea how he had come by it. When we met him he was in his mid-sixties, as far as he could judge. He was exceptionally strong and could carry a two-hundredweight sack of meal, with no apparent effort; as Maud was fond of telling me, 'Jonnie is a very physical man, if you know what I mean! Insists on his conjugal rights at least three times a week!'

We used to love to hear Jonnie's tales of the outback and his early life with the tribe. He knew so much of their folklore and the ways of the bush. He thought he must have been about six or seven when his mother died, her man having been killed in a spear fight some months previously. He had been taken from the small bark hut where they lived by one of the tribal elders, and left in a town, as he 'wasn't really one of them'. Left to fend for himself, he had made his home in the boiler of an abandoned engine and earned a few coppers a day to eke out an existence. He never drank anything but water or soda-pop and ate very sparingly, but his poor beginnings certainly hadn't affected his growth or strength.

The town he had been left in was Kalgoorlie and there was always some odd job to be done for the miners, holding their horses' heads while they bought their provisions and so on. When the Great War came, Jonnie had been in his late teens so he enlisted and was eventually sent to Europe. He served in the trenches and spent several months in England, waiting to be repatriated when the war was over. His sojourn in Europe had left him totally unimpressed with the Western way of life and once back home, he had stayed in West Australia. The next few years were spent as stockman on various stations, leaving only once a year for a holiday in the nearest bush town. It was on one of these visits that he had met Maud.

She had come from a poor London family and in the early 1920s had been given an opportunity to go to Australia and start a new life. The scheme was arranged by a well known charity organisation. The position she had been allocated was as a kitchen maid in a hostel for men and Jonnie had been one of the guests. Most of the men who came there were in town for the usual 'good time' – women, drinking and gambling – but Jonnie, being part native, was not allowed to go into public houses. Aboriginals had no vote and were not allowed to apply for jobs considered 'White Men's Jobs'. The romance had been a very short one and the subsequent marriage controversial. Jonnie had not gone back to his job and presumably Maud had been unable to stay at the hostel, so they had come to Perth to start their life together.

There must have been considerable problems for them; perhaps it was as well there were no children born to them. We always felt that Jonnie must have considered marriage to a white woman quite a step up the social ladder. In spite of his illiteracy, they had become prosperous over the years, no doubt entirely due to Maud's shrewd handling of all money matters. She was a tiny woman, about the same age as Jonnie, shrivelled and brown as a walnut, a cigarette perpetually hanging from her upper lip. She sported a fine nicotine moustache as a result and had one eye always closed against the pungent smoke which drifted endlessly upward. Money was her God and every transaction was meticulously entered in her big ledger. Any small favour Maud did – my cooking or washing arrangements during the house building – merited a price, even if it was only a few shillings at a time.

Jonnie was in many ways 'untamed'. All week he wore only a brief pair of shorts and a singlet, and was always barefoot. On Saturdays, he dressed in a dark suit and a white shirt and put on a pair of shoes. He would set off for town carrying a Gladstone bag, which was called a 'Port' in Australia. We often wondered what he needed one for as he never did any actual shopping. His trips to town were mainly to exchange his well-thumbed comics for more up-to-date ones. There were many 'comic exchange' shops in Perth and weekends were their busiest times. I found it interesting to notice on any train or bus journey the number of adults who would be looking at what we considered children's reading matter. Jonnie always had a pile with him and would sit and chuckle over them like a small child.

One Saturday morning, while on a shopping trip, I came face to face with him in a large chain store like Woolworths. He greeted me pleasantly, patted Vivienne on the head and said, 'How's you going, mate? Busy in here today isn't it?' We were standing beside the tool counter and while he was speaking, his eyes never left my face, but his hands were stealthily filching tools from the counter and dropping them into his open bag!

I was aghast and didn't know how to handle the situation. I mumbled some excuse about being late for the bus, took Vivienne by the hand and fled the scene. This incident explained the rows and rows of tools in his shed and garage, all neatly racked, everything from a screwdriver to a power saw. Ron had borrowed many of them during the house building and whenever he had asked Jonnie if he might have one, he would reply, 'Help yourself mate,' and indicate the rows. He certainly didn't know the names of most of them and we never saw him use a single one! Whether Maud was aware of his magpie habits we don't know.

The summer dragged on with record temperatures and I seemed to exist on salad and endless cups of tea. Cold drinks did nothing to quench my thirst, whereas a cup of really hot tea seemed so refreshing. We were plagued by mosquitoes from the swamp, which left Ron and Vivienne alone but made a meal of me and I began to long for a cooler climate. Coming home from the shop one day, an enormous grasshopper leapt under my skirt and got entangled in my pants. I danced a fandango all down the road, slapping at my thigh, trying to dislodge the creature and feeling its legs pricking my flesh. Indoors I did a strip-tease in record time and was left holding my pants with the remains of its long legs waving at me while its body was squashed all over my thigh. Ugh!

I made up my mind that the Australian way of life wasn't for me and they could keep their great outdoors and all the horrid things that went with it! At the end of two years, we could go home, if Ron agreed. He was his usual understanding self: he felt he could have settled if I had been happy but was quite prepared to return to England and start again if that was what I wanted. We decided that we would need to save a considerable sum of money to pay our fares and so on and that we wouldn't make it by staying in Tinton. The bush was the place to make money, we had been told many times, so we registered with an agency that found positions for single farm hands and hired couples.

Ron had never done any farm work but was strong and willing to learn. Most of the farm jobs had accommodation provided, so we would need to sell our half house. We painted a 'For Sale' sign on a piece of board, hung it outside the door and waited. The very next day an English couple with a seven-year-old son came along and agreed to purchase it. While the legal formalities were being dealt with we received a message from the agency to say a Mr George Price would like to visit us. He had a sheep station some three hundred miles from Perth and needed a married couple to join his staff. He arrived one afternoon and seated himself on one of our small camp chairs. He was a tall, lean man with a leathery face, thinning ginger hair and the coldest blue eyes I have ever seen.

'What experience of farm work do you have?' he asked.

'None at all, but I don't mind hard work or long hours,' Ron replied, and went on to tell him the various jobs he had done. Mr Price told us that a furnished house went with the job, the wage would be fourteen pounds per week and we would have the use of the house cow to provide us with milk. The wage covered the use of my services also, it seemed: the wife of the hired hand was expected to feed any itinerant workers and twenty-five shillings a week would be paid for each man, to cover the cost of the food. It sounded quite a good proposition: no rent to pay, free milk, plenty of wood to fuel the stove, and needless to say, there wouldn't be anywhere to spend our money so we could easily save the fare home.

Ignorance is bliss, so they say, and we shook hands on the deal and agreed to start work for Mr Price in two weeks time, when Ron had worked out his notice at the mill.

'I'll send you directions in a few days' time. Of course, you'll need to find someone to bring you up,' he said. 'It's a pity you haven't got any transport of your own, but there are plenty of vehicles on the farm.'

He left us and we sat planning the amount we thought we could save – what an experience it would be. After all, we would be seeing the real Australia, something not to be missed. Alan agreed to drive us up in his utility truck and we started to pack our boxes. I wrote home, telling the family of our latest plans and giving them the new address. Just Box 24, care of the nearest mail point. On the move, again!

Chapter 12

Outback

The Sunday of the journey was fine but a chill wind was blowing as we piled our belongings into Alan's utility truck. Alan, of course, would be driving, and Annie, his younger daughter, was coming to be company for her father on the long journey back. She sat between me and Alan in the front seat while Ron and Vivienne sat on cushions in the back, facing outward over the tailboard. We had packed sandwiches and flasks of hot drinks because, although we had no way of knowing the conditions we might face, we were sure there would be no cafés on the way!

Once the city was left behind, we passed a shanty town where a number of aboriginal people lived. Their dwellings consisted of shacks constructed from old petrol drums and cans, beaten flat and tacked together, roofed with sheets of rusty corrugated iron. A standpipe stood at either end of the small settlement, where groups of women were waiting to draw water. Swarms of children ran around, barefooted and dressed in a motley collection of cotton dresses, brightly coloured, and cut-down trousers, obviously handed down from older brothers and sisters. They waved and smiled, wide grins showing their strong white teeth and, surrounded by skinny dogs, ran alongside the truck as we drove past. They had a poor existence and I wondered if the tribes who still roamed free and uneducated weren't in many ways better off than these shanty town folks who lived on the fringes of civilisation and sent their children to the mission schools.

We were enveloped in clouds of red dust as we drove on and left the tarmacked roads behind, the hard surfaces giving way to dirt tracks. After about three hours of driving, we stopped for a drink and Ron and Vivienne emerged from the back of the truck. Alan, Annie and I burst out laughing at their appearance. Completely covered in the thick red dust, they looked like a pair of red 'Black and White Minstrels'. Only their eyes and teeth showed white against the red mask.

Annie offered to take a turn in the back and I said I would take Ron's place, although he refused. We didn't stop very long for our break, the swarms of flies and other insects making it too unpleasant, but a slice of cake and a cup of tea was welcome and then we were on our way again. We passed few houses and one or two hamlets with signs exhorting us to 'Please drive carefully' and then, one saloon and petrol pump later, another large sign saying 'Thank you' denoting that we had already left the village.

The trees grew more sparse, the land more desolate. Wire fences lined the roadside with perhaps a few gum trees here and there. Flocks of brilliantly coloured birds flew squawking into the air as we passed, leaving clouds of dust behind us and the dove-grey galahs, with their rose pink breasts, perched on the fences in rows, like spectators at a race course. We halted for a lunch break but again, the insects prevented us from enjoying it and it was useless to sit down. We were soon on our way again and in the late afternoon, we saw a rough signpost to Binnie, the nearest settlement to Korrine, which was our future home. Binnie boasted a saloon bar, complete with a hitching rail and a swinging door, just like something from a Western movie, a general store which also served as a post office, and a butcher's shop. There were only a handful of dwellings but the surrounding sheep stations no doubt kept the traders in business with their weekly purchases. As it was a Sunday the place was deserted and we drove on until a gate bearing a board proclaimed this was Korrine land.

For the next few miles, I leapt in and out of the truck, opening and shutting numerous gates, although the sheep some distance away showed no interest in our presence. The track wound on and on, the clouds of dust obscuring our view at times. I gazed around in amazement, not a blade of grass in sight, only a few bare stunted trees and the metal windmills for drawing up the water breaking up the monotony of the landscape. It was no wonder the sheep nearest to us looked so skinny. A brown cattle dog came streaking toward us through the dust, barking hysterically and trying to bite the wheels, causing Alan to brake sharply so that we swerved off the track. He reversed and drove slowly forward, the dog still frantically attacking the wheels, and as the dust began to clear, we saw ahead the huge iron sheds, a couple of asbestos shacks and, away to the right, a large brick-built bungalow. We had arrived!

Alan stopped the truck outside the bungalow and Ron and I dismounted and knocked on the door. A woman in her mid-fifties answered it. She was tall and heavily built, with white hair, tightly permed, and her skin had the lined weather-beaten texture of so many Australian women.

'Come in, you must be Ron and Kathleen,' she said. 'My husband is away over the other side of Binnie.'

We entered a spacious kitchen. A fridge, run on kerosene, dominated one wall, a table and four chairs another and the usual wood stove occupied the third wall; a window and door looked across the sand at the vast empty spaces of the bush. She didn't ask us to sit down or offer us any refreshment and we stood there awkwardly. She finished putting away some dishes she had evidently just washed and said, 'Right, if you'll follow me, I'll show you the house.'

Ron and I followed her out of the house and across the sand while Alan drove behind. The two small dwellings we had noticed as we arrived were some two hundred yards from the main house. We passed the first one, which was apparently occupied as the window was open and curtains hung there. She halted in front of the smaller one and opened the door. I don't quite know what I expected but it certainly wasn't this. We had been told a furnished house went with the job, but as Mrs Price opened the door, the only furniture to be seen was a ricketty table.

There was a bedroom with a narrow room adjoining it. 'Your second bedroom,' she said, with a wave of her hand. It had a slit window and a concrete floor and could more properly be described as a cell. Our room had a board floor and some nails in the wooden struts to hang clothes on. Nothing else. Likewise the living room, an open grate and a board floor. The kitchen contained the old table and a wood stove. A tap protruded from one wall but there was no sink. We stood, speechless, until Mrs Price spoke, 'I'll leave you to unpack your things and light your stove; you'll find mallee roots outside for fuel, chop some more when you need it,' and as she turned to leave she added, 'You'll be able to start feeding the men tomorrow.'

I found my voice. 'Not until I get some furniture,' I said. 'Mr Price said we would have a furnished house to live in. Where would anyone sit if I was cooking meals for them? Come to that, where will we sleep?' I spoke firmly. The fact that we had brought our flock mattress with us was neither here nor there.

She was totally uninterested. 'Oh, I expect we shall find you a few bits and pieces; you can start cooking on Tuesday. That will give you plenty of time to sort yourselves out.' She marched away across the sand, back to her large brick bungalow.

I felt utterly dejected – miles and miles of seemingly barren land, thousands and thousands of scrawny sheep and a woman who struck me as being as hard as her husband. Ron and Alan unloaded the truck and carried our possessions in: the huge trunk containing our linen, clothes and pillows; the boxes which held our food and utensils; our mattress; and the little camp bed we had bought for Vivienne when we built our half house. We couldn't offer Alan and Annie any food or even a drink as we knew it would take some time to get the stove going.

With a long journey ahead, Alan was anxious to be on his way. We said our 'Goodbyes' and watched them disappear up the dusty track, the brown dog once again barking at the wheels just as he had been less than an hour before when we arrived. It was no use standing around: here we were and here we would have to stay for the foreseeable future.

We lit the stove, using some of the huge misshapen roots which we learned later were often dug up during ploughing, remnants of some age past when the ground had been one vast forest. An enormous axe stood outside the door, and it certainly needed the blade of this monster to make any impression on the mallee roots, for they were iron hard. I filled a kettle from the one tap, noticing that it was fed from a rainwater tank at the back of the house. Also at the back was a tiny bathroom with a chipped old bath and a funnel-shaped boiler, of the kind we had used at Mrs Shales'. The privy stood some way across the sand, just a hole in the ground with a primitive seat of asbestos. That, at least, would be no hardship – it had become the normal toilet by this time. It took only a few minutes to unpack our bed linen and make up the camp bed in the cell room and our mattress on the floor; our clothes we hung on the nails available. The little camp table and folding chairs were set around the living room, looking quite lost on the bare boards. Our few pictures were hung and our few books we placed on the window-sill. There was nothing else to do; most of our belongings would have to stay in the trunk until Mr Price provided some kind of furniture. The food stayed in the boxes – there was nowhere else to put them, in the absence of even one cupboard. We ate the sandwiches that were left over and had a cup of tea and decided we might just as well go to bed. As there were no chairs, we sat on our boxes. We didn't talk very much; it all felt like disaster with a capital D. The dusk fell suddenly as it always did and a generator sprang into life over in one of the big sheds. At least we had electricity, even if it was only for a few hours each day. Tired out with the journey and certainly depressed at the situation we seemed to be in, we put Vivienne to bed and undressed ourselves. A moon was rising and as we lay on our mattress we could see it through the grimy window. There were no curtains, of course, but somewhere in the big box I knew I had a pair. Tomorrow we could make the place look a little more like home.

Ron spoke. 'Well, do you think we've made yet another mistake?'

'Job to say, I suppose we shall get used to it – won't seem half as bad when we get a few chairs and a cupboard or two,' I replied.

'I have to start work at seven in the morning. I think I had better set the alarm clock. We shall need to be up at five if we want a hot drink – that stove will take at least an hour to get really hot,' said Ron.

I sighed. I could see the cooking arrangements being quite a problem. The alarm clock was set and I placed a torch by the mattress in case we had to get up during the night, and we settled down.

I fell into a deep sleep, no doubt dreaming my recurring dream, in which I walked down the pavements of my old road, seeing so plainly every crack and kerbstone. I awoke suddenly, aware that something strange had disturbed me. We had noticed that there were no locks on the doors but I supposed that there were hardly likely to be many visitors in this isolated spot. I sat up and listened: there was a peculiar noise, a kind of scraping sound.

'Ron, wake up, I think we may have an intruder.' I prodded him gently. He sat up.

'I think you're right. It's outside though. Pass the torch and I'll have a look.'

He crept across the room and carefully opened the window, switching on the torch, although the moon was high by now and lit up the ground clearly. An enormous kangaroo was simply scratching his back on the side of the house and, startled by the beam of the torch, hopped rapidly away, his huge feet leaving imprints in the sand. We both stood at the window, looking after the animal as he went towards the distant gum trees. They were etched starkly against a sky as dark and smooth as velvet, sequinned by the unfamiliar stars of the Southern Hemisphere.

'You have to admit that this landscape has a beauty all of its own,' Rob said.

I agreed, but as I settled back on the mattress, I thought with longing of our damp little basement flat in England. Maybe distance does lend enchantment, but at that moment, England felt like Paradise.

Chapter 13

Korrine

We were up at dawn the next morning, lit the stove, ate our breakfast and by seven a.m. Ron was across at the cow-shed to learn how to milk the two cows. We had not seen anyone on the farm the previous day; I had assumed that being a Sunday, everyone had gone into town – the nearest real town, some sixty-five miles distant. Looking over towards the sheds in the early morning I could see several men and Mr Price towering above them all. I saw him greet Ron and go with him in the direction of a tin hut which I learned later was the cow-shed. Daisy and Bess, the two cows, gave sufficient milk for the needs of all the farm workers and often, enough to make cream. Daisy was a gentle Jersey cow, who was in calf and would soon 'go dry' and would not be milked again until she dropped her calf. I would love to have been at the shed that first morning for, although Ron was familiar with cattle, having lived near a farm as a child, he had never actually handled one. He was a 'natural' Mr Price told him; in fact he could not believe it was the first time Ron had touched a cow.

Half an hour later, Ron returned to the house carrying a stainless steel pail of warm, steaming milk. Vivienne consented to drink a glass, grimacing as she put down the empty vessel, and said, 'Well, I don't think much of that. I would sooner have that "apologised" stuff we get in the town!' I must confess I didn't like it much either. I used to make cream which we all enjoyed, and found plenty of uses for it in cooking, milk puddings and so on, but only Ron would drink it for pleasure.

Later that day our 'furniture' arrived: a rough bench for sitting on and a table top with iron legs, which had been made that day in the workshop.

There was no doubt that Mr Price was a very successful farmer: there were a dozen vehicles at Korrine, trucks and cars, every mechanical device imaginable to keep the equipment in good working order, even their own petrol pump. The sheds were very up-to-date and anything needed for the farm could be made on the premises. Also, of course, there were the huge tractors and harvesters.

I had the table placed in the kitchen and the old one removed; our tiny camp table and chairs from Perth which were in the living room, were strong enough for Vivienne and me but they would not sustain the weight of a man. Some weeks later an old bedstead was acquired but that was the sum total of our furniture. Ron built a wide shelf along the kitchen wall, under the tap, so that I could use it as a work surface and our boxes of food stood underneath.

Mrs Price called on me that afternoon to see how I had settled in and to tell me that next day four men would arrive to do the 'crutching'.

'The sheep need all the loose wool cut away from their hind quarters before lambing starts,' she said. 'You'll be able to cook for the men now that you have a table; they have their breakfast at seven a.m., cake and tea up at the sheds at ten thirty, dinner at one o'clock and their evening meal at seven.' She turned to go and then, as an afterthought, 'Oh, a billy can of tea and cake at the shed at three thirty.' She stared at me for a moment, as I stood, mouth open in astonishment. 'What's the matter?'

'I haven't got enough food to feed four men,' I gasped, 'and I don't have any billy cans.'

She seemed surprised. 'I'll get George to take Ron into Binnie to stock up. You'll get twenty-five shillings per man per week so you'll do all right. They only take about a week over the crutching.'

As she started to walk across the sand, a girl came out of the other house, to hang some washing on a small line. Mrs Price paused, said something to her and turned, coming back to me with the girl following. 'Here's Kathleen, you might as well meet her now,' she said, indicating me.

The girl was in her mid-twenties, dark-haired and with enormous brown eyes.

'This is Sally,' Mrs Price waved a hand towards her as if she were an object. 'Of course, that isn't her name really, they have such ridiculous names we can't be bothered with them. We call them Bill and Sally. I'll leave you to get to know each other. I'll go and find George and organise those stores.'

She went off in the direction of the sheds and Sally and I stood looking at each other. Sally looked over her shoulder at the retreating figure with an expression of intense dislike. I spoke first. 'My name is Kathleen Upton, this is my daughter, Vivienne. I'm sorry Mrs Price spoke about you like that. I'm sure we can pronounce your names all right.'

She smiled. 'It is no matter; we understand. We are Cornelius and Hendrikus, but all here say Bill and Sally, you do the same.' She shrugged her shoulders. 'You are to feed the men tomorrow, yes?'

I explained about the crutching team arriving and asked how many people were living here or employed on the farm. She counted out on her fingers, 'Mr Price, Mrs Price, their youngest son, Roy; he is horrible, so like his father. They have a girl, Nell, she is married to another farmer and lives away, she don't come often. The oldest son, he also has a farm, but very far. Sometimes he comes with a . . . a . . . plane.' Her English was quite good and by her accent I knew she was from Holland and was surprised when she told me she had only been here about eight months. 'Then there is Wolfgang.' Her tone was bitter. 'He is a German and we have to feed him in our kitchen. The Prices do not understand our hatred, but now you feed him, yes?'

'I expect so, when the crutchers have gone. Anyone else?'

'Yes, one boy, Len. He is a friend of the family, I think. His parents used to farm near here and he is learning to be a farmer too.'

'Does he live in the house with the Prices?'

'Not at all, he and Wolf live over there.' She pointed in the opposite direction to the cluster of sheds. There was a low concrete building with an iron roof.

'All the men workers sleep there but we have to cook their food. It is a place only for their sleeping and washing and such.'

We chatted for a little while and I liked her immediately. I sensed that she was unhappy at Korrine and that the presence of a German in her own home distressed her. Ron came running back to the house just then to get some money for stores; he was off to Binnie with Mr Price.

'How are you?' I asked, 'I haven't seen you all day.'

He grinned. 'OK I suppose. I've been spreading fertiliser ready for the sowing; so far I've lost my pen, my hat and my watch!'

I couldn't help laughing at his expression.

'Don't you know where you've lost them?'

'Oh yes, down that huge hopper and into the ground somewhere. I'll never see them again, worse luck.'

Needless to say, he never did. The moral of that story was never to have anything in the pockets of overalls when spreading fertiliser. He went off in a truck, returning at dusk, leaving me to unpack the box of goods while he went to milk the cows.

I unpacked the goods, taking out the things I wanted for the evening meal and re-packed the rest into the boxes, there being nowhere else to put them. Ron had brought some fish for the main course, frozen, and there on the carton was 'Produced in Grimsby'. How strange that my first cooked meal in the bush should have come more than twelve thousand miles, from home! It was after seven when Ron came in for dinner, tired out. It had been a very long day.

I spent the next morning baking cakes ready for the arrival of the crutchers: if there were four men with hearty appetites needing cake twice a day, heaven knew how much they would consume. Ron had brought a joint of beef from the butcher in Binnie, but I decided not to put it in the oven until I saw the men arrive. In the event, it was dark when I heard a truck rattling down the track and the headlights lit up the room as it swept past, the brown dog barking at the wheels as usual. Roy Price came across to say the men had eaten already and would not require a meal but would be in for their breakfast at seven a.m.

Next morning Ron was still milking the cows when the crutchers appeared at our door. I had put cornflakes and fruit juice on the table which they declined, so I poured them tea and prepared the scrambled eggs and toast. There was also plenty of bread and butter, jam and marmalade. I placed a plate in front of each of them with three slices of toast apiece and an enormous pile of scrambled egg. There was dead silence. Vivienne paused, a spoonful of flakes poised in mid-air. I waited, wondering what was wrong. Then the eldest of the men spoke.

'And what the hell you do call that bloody mess?'

'Why, it's scrambled egg,' I said brightly.

'Well, you know what you can do with your bloody scrambled egg, missus,' he told me. The other three grunted agreement and the plates were pushed away. They consumed more than a loaf between them of bread and jam, drank several cups of tea each and stood up from the table. The smallest man with weasel-like features and mean little eyes set close together said, 'We want strong tea and slabs of cake mid-morning up at the shed, missus, and I might as well tell you now, we eat meat for breakfast, mid-day and dinner at night. If we don't get it we down shears and move on.' He gave a derisive sniff and left with his mates to go to the bunkhouse and collect their tools.

Ron came in to snatch a hurried breakfast before going out with the dogs to round up the first flock ready for the crutchers. 'Whatever is the matter?' he wanted to know, seeing Vivienne and me still sitting at the table, surrounded by the plates of congealing eggs. I told him and we couldn't help seeing the funny side of it – my idea of a good breakfast and theirs was totally at odds. The dogs gobbled up the rejected food with obvious relish, so it wasn't all wasted.

What on earth shall I give them at lunch time? I'll cook the beef for tonight but I can see that disappearing in one sitting,' I said.

'Goodness knows. I can't get back to Binnie today; I've left an order at the store but he won't be here until Friday; he brings the goods, a weekly paper and any mail then.' He turned to go, 'Can you rustle up something that looks like meat, do you think?'

'I'll try,' I said, having a sinking feeling that catering for this uncouth bunch was going to present a number of problems.

'Perhaps you can get a rabbit tonight if it's not too dark when you come in.'

When Ron had gone I cleared up and ransacked my box of stores. I found my largest roasting pan and emptied into it tins of spaghetti, baked beans, mixed vegetables and two tins of corned beef. I topped it with sliced potato and grated cheese. I hoped it would be eatable as I put it in the oven. At mid-morning Vivienne and I went up to the sheds with two huge billy cans of tea and slices of fruit cake. Ron had purchased the cans in Binnie the day before, made of metal with tight-fitting lids and handles to carry them by. They held about a gallon each. The men worked to a strict schedule, two hours each stint and then a break. At lunch time they arrived, sweaty and unwashed, and ravenous. I served the hash with salad and hunks of bread and, to my surprise, they enjoyed it. Willy, the weasel, somewhat shamefaced, said, 'Gee, missus, that was beaut, would you give me the recipe sometime, then my old woman can make it!'

I was so taken aback that I couldn't think what to say. I think he must have been sorry about the breakfast time fiasco.

Our days settled into a routine of seemingly endless work. Each evening Ron would have to slaughter a sheep, selected by the crutchers. This was the usual procedure with them – naturally they chose the sheep with the most meat on it. It was a job he hated for he had to cut the poor animal's throat, skin it and leave it to hang in the little stone building that served as our laundry. It would be jointed the next day, some of it going to Sally to feed her small crew, some of it for the Prices and the rest for me, to feed the largest number. Chops for breakfast, cold mutton and soup for mid-day and a roast meal at night. The billy can and cake routine twice a day, the cleaning and washing (thank goodness I didn't have to wash for the men) – I began to see why the married couples never stayed very long. I wasn't on the payroll but my day was as hard as Ron's. Sally and I became good friends; as I had thought, she hated the bush life and she and Bill were planning to go back to the town as soon as they could. Their hatred of Wolf was ever apparent. Bill was always muttering, 'One day I will keel him, I hate him so bad.' He told us how he had been in the Dutch Resistance during the war and of the dreadful times they had endured, culminating in months of near starvation towards the end, when the Allies were fighting on their soil. In spite of all the years since then, it is noticeable whenever we go to Holland that there is no love lost between the Dutch people and their erstwhile enemies, even now.

The crutching lasted about ten days and the men departed, no doubt to head for town and drink the proceeds of their labours. Sally told Mrs Price that she would no longer feed Wolf in her house, so I gained two more mouths to feed, both Len and Wolf. I soon found the twenty-five shillings per week allocated for each man's board totally inadequate: we were hopelessly out of pocket. Every item of food delivered to the farm carried a freight charge, which made the food so expensive. Our dreams of saving a large sum of money while in the bush began to fade.

I enrolled Vivienne in the Australian School of Correspondence as she was five years old and I felt she needed to start her education. A roll of lessons would arrive each Friday and the mailman would take away the completed lessons. So, added to all my other tasks, I had to fit in a timetable of school hours and supervise her work. We had no radio or telephone, unlike the 'School of the Air' which I understand gets splendid results. It was quite difficult to follow the syllabus because Vivienne learned so quickly. The books which should have taken a whole term to read were completed in a fortnight. We had always read to her a great deal, both stories and poems, being bookworms ourselves, and in two weeks she was able to read any of the children's books we possessed. I improvised and invented a number of lessons to capture her interest. When school was over for the day she would go off into the bush, taking a doll or her teddy with her, or play games outside on the sand. She would assemble her entire family of animals and dolls and conduct an orchestra, making all the appropriate gestures and musical noises. I have never known her ask, 'What can I do now, Mum?' as so many children do. There were no other playmates for her but being alone all the time did not seem to worry her at all.

Sally was a devout Catholic, unlike Bill, who paid only lip-service to their religion. She had an enormous crucifix on the bedroom wall and several times each day she would kneel and pray. The house was spotlessly clean, always smelt of polish and soap, and faintly of the incense she used in her little shrine. She told me proudly that the cross had been the one which had lain on her father's coffin before his funeral. It was one of her most treasured possessions. She derived great comfort from her devotions but Bill told us once, 'Sally, she don't see me with my eyes open or she go mad. I mumble but I don't know what she saying. The Holy Father, he just a man.' He would pull a face and shrug his shoulders as if to say that was that. Bill was a likeable man but when roused he had a flaming temper. He detested both Mr and Mrs Price, who were as hard as I had suspected, as was their son: mean in so many ways. For instance, if we wanted some eggs from the hens, we had to pay the shop price for them, this in spite of the fact that feeding the birds most days was one of my jobs!

One day after Bill had yet another disagreement with Mrs Price, he had stormed over to us, followed as usual by an anxious Sally. 'That Meeses Price,' he raged, 'I wish that she may die in the "sheet" house.'

'You must not say that,' pleaded Sally, 'It is wicked and it isn't the "sheet" house, I have told you, it is called the "toilet".'

'Well, toilet or sheet house, it is all the same to me, it is the worst place she can have died,' he muttered. He never got his wish – Mrs Price lived to be quite old but did, in the end, have a very painful death.

The wet season arrived and day after day the rain poured down, Ron, Bill, Wolf and Len were on the tractors all day now, for it was almost sowing time. The tractors had no cabs for shelter and they would drape sacks round their shoulders to try and keep dry. Mr Price used to say, 'I don't want to hear those tractors stop until sundown,' and he would patrol the miles of paddocks in a truck, carrying with him a pair of powerful binoculars through which he would peer to make sure they were working hard enough. He certainly wanted his pound of flesh!

The rains lasted about six or seven weeks and then stopped abruptly. Blades of grass peeped through the barren ground; in a week the sand was covered in wild flowers and grasses. Spring had sprung!

Chapter 14

Springtime

The flowers were a picture, yellow, white, blue and pink, none of them known to us. Some of them were perfumed, delicate-looking plants; the ground was covered, every grain of sand obscured by this blanket of colour. On Mr Price's orders Ron had put a wire fence around the patch of sand referred to as our 'garden'. Several ewes in lamb were put inside to eat the grass. The reason for this was so that there would be no place for snakes to hide. As the weather grew warmer they would be coming out of their sleep and we knew there were nests under the house. If the grass was kept really short it gave us a chance to avoid treading on them. Since we had been told that all the snakes in that part of Australia were poisonous we weren't taking any risks.

The yellow flowers were similar to our horse daisies but they had an unfortunate effect on us: they made us sneeze continually. Pretty as they were to look at I wasn't sorry when their blooming season was over. In a few weeks they had all withered and it wasn't long before the grass died too. Then it was back to the barren landscape as before, until the wheat began to peep through. As it grew it was almost like the sea; if ruffled by a breeze it would ripple and I could close my eyes and imagine it was the English Channel. Ron continued to work very long hours and there was no mention of a half day, although we had been told that Saturdays were a half day and Sundays a complete day off. It was a busy time. With the sheep about to lamb some of them were rounded up and brought nearer to the farm but with thousands of ewes there were still miles to travel to watch over them. That year was a bad time as several years of drought had left them in poor condition to bear their lambs.

90

When the short period of grass growing was over they had to be fed with a kind of oats. Vivienne and I would often go with Ron while he drove slowly over the paddocks, Vivienne and I sitting in the back of the truck with sacks of fodder, letting it dribble out as we criss-crossed the ground. The poor skinny beasts would come running at the sound of the vehicle, bleating so piteously as they crowded around, each trying to get a good share of the food. It was the first time for over thirty years that farmers in that area had ever had to hand feed. Although the ground always looked so barren there was a kind of clover seed deep in the earth which could grow in any conditions, and it was this which sustained them.

With the two cows it was a different matter. Daisy was no longer milked as she was near to calving, so after Bess had been seen to in the morning both cows were turned loose into the bush to find what food they could. They would wander for miles, stopping only when they could not physically go further, being prevented by wire fences. At dusk it was often my task to go out and find them and bring them in. Daisy never wanted to come, I think she just wanted to be left in peace to give birth to her calf. But one cow wouldn't come without the other and I would get behind them, pushing, shoving and shouting and practically manhandle them back to the shed. Daisy eventually gave birth to a sturdy little bull calf and it was heartrending when, in less than a week, it was taken away from her to be hand-reared and sold. For days she lowed incessantly, not moving from her shed, eating very little and making Bess as miserable as herself. Finally she gave up and went back into the bush daily, giving her creamy milk again for our use. Within a month it was time for Bess to be put to the bull and the whole process started over again.

As the lambing started so did the blowflies. It is difficult to explain to anyone who has not experienced it what a nightmare it can be. I suppose the people who are born in the bush are used to it, but to someone brought up to believe that blowflies are disgusting, germ-carrying creatures, it was horrifying.

Indoors they made life impossible, thousands of them swarming around from daylight to dusk, filling the air with their loud buzzing and, worst of all, zooming over us and ejecting their maggots as they flew. Unlike our English bluebottles, who lay eggs, their maggots were fully-grown grubs, who would crawl rapidly off in all directions. We used a spray gun on them and ordered several canisters of the foul-smelling liquid each week. I remember one day writing to my mother, sitting at the kitchen table, brushing up the maggots every few minutes from the table and floor, spraying again, brushing up again, and almost in tears at the sheer futility of it all. As they crawled all over the air letter, dying flies ejecting the grubs over the page, I thought 'How could I possibly tell them this at home; they would have to see it to believe it.'

Although we had fly wires over the door, windows and even the chimney, it made no difference; the walls did not quite reach the ground and I assume they came underneath. The mice certainly did and in the evenings when we sat down for a few minutes respite after our meal, we frequently had to get up and chase the mice from our food boxes. They nibbled their way through packets of flour, rice and lentils, or cornflakes, which was their favourite, and anything in a bag. Annoying as this was, in no way did it bother me like the blowflies. Mrs Price called one afternoon and said, 'Thought I'd better warn you, if you feel something crawling up your legs, make sure it's not a blowfly.'

'What do you mean?' I asked.

'Well, they'll blow you in the crutch the same as they will the sheep,' she said, 'I've been blown a number of times, it's difficult to get at the little blighters once they've gone up inside.' I was horrified; the thought of maggots in my inside or Vivienne's appalled me. When Ron came in that night I told him, my voice squeaking with near hysteria. He couldn't understand it. 'What's all the panic for, where are all these flies you keep telling me about, I can't see any. You should be outside all day and have to contend with those damned little sand flies,' he said.

'Of course you never see them, they come with the daylight and disappear with the dusk, I don't know where they go. One day, if you ever get a day off, stay indoors and you'll see plenty of them!' I shouted.

It was only a few days later that Mr Price actually gave the men a day off. It was a Sunday, although Ron still had to do the milking, but when he returned for his breakfast he couldn't believe what he saw. We had to shout to make ourselves heard above the noise of buzzing and, after the first spraying, he swept a cornflake box full of dead flies off the kitchen windowsill alone. 'I never dreamed it was like this,' he kept saying, 'I wish I had shares in the fly spray company. We must spend pounds on the stuff.' We did, and it is said that the man that can invent something to wipe out the flies in the bush will be a millionaire overnight. I believe it!

There were no more days off for a long time. The lambing was in full swing now with dreadful loss of both ewes and lambs. The ewes were so weak they had difficulty in giving birth and all too often, the moment the lambs' heads were visible, the ever-hovering crows would swoop down and peck their eyes out. The lambs would die, and more often than not, the mothers too. School lessons were abandoned and Vivienne went with Ron in the truck each day, her sharp eyes spotting ewes in trouble before Ron.

He kept a large pot of petroleum jelly in the truck and got used to the cry, 'Daddy, over there, I think you'll need the Vaseline again,' as he prepared to act as midwife to yet another ewe in distress.

Hundreds of lambs and ewes died. A number of the little motherless creatures were brought to the farm and Mrs Price, Sally and I did our best to keep them alive. I raised two in the end, dear little beasts; we called them Larry and Laddie. Born to separate mothers, they were so different in both appearance and character that I wondered why people always think sheep look alike. Larry was a short fat lamb, while Laddie had long legs, a thinner face and was very greedy. They were bottle fed and as the cows' milk was not of sufficient yield to feed the farmworkers and the lambs we had to buy drums of powdered milk from the stores at Binnie. Laddie was always fed first as he seemed ravenous, then he would saunter off, pretending he wasn't interested any more. He would wait until Larry had a firm grip on the teat of the bottle and was enjoying his feed, then turn and thunder down the sand, knock poor Larry flying and grab the bottle, guzzling furiously until I could wrest it away from him. Just like a naughty child. Vivienne loved them. Where she went, they followed; indoors or out, they became her constant playmates. One of their favourite ploys was to follow us to the privy. Because of the possibility of snakes we were advised to carry a length of rubber hose with us. The procedure was as follows. First, kick the door open and stand well back to see if a snake slithers out. If so, give it a hefty whack with the hose. Thank goodness I never had to put it to the test, but I was assured that the hose-pipe would kill them, whereas a stick would simply break. I never allowed Vivienne to go on her own. There were often redbacks in the pan and we couldn't take chances; the nearest doctor was some sixty miles away and we had no transport of our own. Nor, of course, was there a telephone on the farm. Larry and Laddie loved to come to the privy because they had discovered that toilet paper made a tasty snack.

They would crowd in behind Vivienne and me and start snatching off the sheets, pushing each other and trying to get the largest possible number in their mouths at one time. In the end we had to shoo them out as, apart from the cost of toilet paper, I didn't consider it was suitable fare for lambs. Laddie also had a nasty habit of sneaking to the rear of the pan and taking a sly nip of the available bottom! We were really sad when they were several months old and, having been shorn and castrated, had to rejoin the flock.

Bluey, the old sheep dog, wasn't very well at the time. She was almost fourteen years old and had a large growth in her stomach. She quickly got out of breath and Ron would often lift her into the back of the truck for a ride, while Vivienne and I did the running. I enjoyed the round-ups. It was better than being indoors facing the dreaded blowflies. One of the 'perks' given to the married couple was collecting what the farmers called the 'dead wool'. When a ewe died, if it could be found quickly, the wool could be plucked, in the same way that you pluck a hen. If it was more than about twenty-four hours, it was impossible to do that, but the carcase could be left until the carrion and foxes had eaten the flesh, then the fleece could be salvaged. Bill and Sally were not included in this 'deal'. They had by now given a month's notice and were going down to Perth to try their luck. They hoped to rent a room and, if possible, to get jobs nearby to save their fare to return to Holland. I dreaded them going, for Sally was the only person I had to talk to, apart from Ron and Vivienne. Mrs Price didn't have much to say to me; it was strictly a boss and hired hand relationship. Mr Price and I had little in common either. He came to see me one day and said, accusingly,

'You've been feeding the dogs again, haven't you?'

I agreed that I had. In fact I gave both dogs a bowl of bread and milk each morning, and any scraps I could find.

'Well I forbid you to do it any more,' he said.

I felt my hackles rise. 'You forbid me, why?'

'The bitch is useless, she is too lazy to round up the sheep any more, and the other one has never been any good. Don't think I don't know about the truck rides while you do the running.'

I spoke sharply, 'She is old and sick, she's served you faithfully for years, don't you think she deserves a peaceful retirement? The other one, maybe he is a little mad but he's harmless.'

'Up here, the rule is, if you don't work you don't eat.' His voice was cold.

'It's a poor look out for us then, what happens if one of us is taken ill? I shall go on feeding them as long as I choose. I pay for the food, you don't.'

I shut the door, furious at his attitude. Such a lot of the farmers, it seemed, cared nothing for the animals; they only saw them as so many pounds and pence. Most nights after dark we took the small truck out and went 'wool gathering'. We had to pay Mr Price for the use of it and for the petrol we used and, of course, it had to be in our own time. It was a filthy, smelly business. We would drive over the paddocks, stopping wherever we saw a dead sheep and drag them into piles. I would hold a torch while Ron plucked those newly dead, then we would hide the others in the scrub for a few days until we could salvage the fleeces. The smell was atrocious and often as you touched a sheep it would baa and sigh, just as if it were still alive, as the gases escaped.

The body would be moving sometimes and we would pause, then realise it was the millions of maggots that physically moved the carcase. Vivienne was always with us on these expeditions as we couldn't leave her alone in the house, and from that time onward she refused to eat meat. She is still a vegetarian and feels that unless she were prepared to kill an animal for food she had no right to eat it. We ourselves do eat meat, though not a lot, but on the rare occasions we have lamb I try not to think about those days. All our dead wool was baled up and stored in one of the sheds, ready for transporting to the auction rooms later, after the shearing. Our name was stencilled on the outside and we raised almost two hundred pounds at the sale towards our fare home. I felt we had more than earned it!

When the lambing was over Bill and Sally departed. They had arranged to pay for a lift with a truck driver who was delivering some equipment to Korrine and returning to Perth. Like us, they had no real furniture, although their house was properly furnished. It even had rugs on the floors and a kerosene cooker as well as the wood stove. Sally had made it very homely with Delft ware, Dutch paintings and all sorts of knick-knacks brought from Holland. She had a beautiful grandmother clock which had been in her family for years and some lovely hand-crocheted bedspreads. They were going to travel light, she told me, and wondered if we would like to buy her pots and pans, etc. If they could get work together in a hotel, living in, they would only need their personal items.

I agreed; we didn't have many belongings and all the items would be useful, so we fixed a price. Bill came over the evening before they left and asked Ron to help him carry the box. It was enormous, a strong wooden crate that had been especially made for them to journey to Australia. There were pots and pans, plates and dishes, cutlery, including all sort of implements I had never seen before, and a small piano accordion! I had not seen either Bill or Sally play on it but there it was, in the 'Dutch Box' as we called it. We had that box long after we came home, so much could be packed into it, and though the box itself has gone I still use some of Sally's pans today.

She came across with Bill to say a tearful goodbye. She was clutching the huge cross which had graced her father's coffin. 'Would you please have this, Kathleen, as a remembrance from me,' she begged. I didn't like to refuse it as I knew how much it meant to her, so I thanked her and took it from her arms. It felt as if it weighed a ton, solid mahogany and a silver crucifix screwed on the front. I actually kept it for many years and finally gave it to a friend who was trying to refurbish a little chapel. She was delighted with it and as far as I know it still hangs there.

They left early the next morning, sitting up in front of the truck, their few belongings rolled up in their bedding, waving to us as they disappeared in a cloud of dust up the track. There was a rather sad end to their journey, we learned from the truck driver next time he came to Korrine. He had left the dirt roads and was driving quite fast along the main highway when their roll of belongings came loose, fell off into the road and was run over by a large truck following them. The ornaments, the Delft plates, the glass and china were all smashed, the lovely clock crushed beyond recognition. The glass had cut their clothes and bedding to ribbons and they had nothing left but the clothes they stood up in. I felt so sorry for them but felt thankful that, at least, her precious cross was safe.

I had hoped that with Bill and Sally gone we could have moved into the nicer house. It would have been so much more comfortable but Mrs Price soon let me know that Len's parents would be arriving shortly to give a hand with the shearing. They had always remained friends and sometimes came up to Korrine to help out. So we carried on as we were, Wolf and Len still boarding with us and sleeping in the bunk house. Len was a quiet boy, eating his meals and departing to do his washing and other chores, but Wolf liked to stay for a chat.

His manners were impeccable. He always stood up when I entered the room and clicked his heels and bowed when he left the house. We never knew how old he was. He was very careful when he spoke about the war, saying, 'I was just a little boy at the time.' One day he brought a photo album to show us some pictures of his family. As he turned one page there was a picture of himself in Nazi uniform, standing to attention beside a tank. Without thinking, I exclaimed, 'You, Wolf! In that uniform!'

'No, no, it is not me, it is my cousin,' he said quickly.

We never saw the album again and I thought of Bill who used to say, 'Look at him, on that tractor. Take off his hat and put a square helmet on him, can't you think he is driving a tank!' It was true; he looked every inch a soldier.

We had a few quiet days after the lambing and even had a weekend off. Everyone on the farm went into town to a film show. It turned out to be an advertising feature about Shell petrol, but at least was a break in routine. Shearing was about to start, the team would soon be arriving, the endless cooking would be my lot again. I hoped the men would be a little less rough than the previous ones, but I would soon find out!

Chapter 15

The Shearing

We were told that the shearing would start on a Monday and I could expect the men to arrive on the Sunday evening, so they would require breakfast on the following morning. Apparently they were not the same team as the crutchers, for which I was thankful. Len's parents were expected on the Saturday so Len would not be eating with us while his parents were there; even so, with Wolf and the four shearers and ourselves there would still be eight for each meal. Quite a crowd in our tiny kitchen. Ron was over at the milking shed on the Sunday morning when I went out to the wood-pile for some more mallee roots. A man was coming across the sand, carrying a milking pail and heading towards the other cottage. There had been a heavy frost during the night and it was still cold. He was wearing an overcoat and a balaclava helmet and, perched on top of this, a trilby hat. He stopped beside me and setting down his pail, he raised his hat.

'Good morning, isn't it a nippy one?' He spoke with an English accent laced with 'Strine'. 'I'm Edward, Len's father, you must be Kathleen. I understand you have been feeding my boy very well.'

He held out his hand and we shook hands. It was so long since anyone had raised their hat to me or greeted me as if I were a lady that my eyes filled with tears. That was the beginning of a friendship with Edward and Wilma, his wife, that lasted until Edward died, several years ago. He had actually been born in Sussex and emigrated to Australia with his parents when he was sixteen. His father had been one of a large family, most of whom had set sail for the continent after the first world war. Edward had married a girl born of Scottish parents; they had two fine sons and had farmed near Korrine for some years. They now lived and worked in the city, returning to help their old neighbours from time to time. To the end of his days Edward remained very English and told us often that, if it hadn't been for his two sons and later his grandchildren, he would have retired to spend his last years 'back home' as he always called it.

We spent a few moments chatting and Wilma came out to greet me, a pleasant fresh-faced woman. Her parents had met while on board ship sailing to their new country and married soon after landing. That was one shipboard romance that lasted a lifetime. Wilma told me they expected to stay about six weeks until the shearing was finished and all the bales dispatched to the salerooms at Fremantle. The truck bearing the shearers arrived at dusk and judging from the sounds drifting across from the bunk house they had spent a very merry weekend indeed. I didn't serve scrambled egg for breakfast this time; mutton chops and fried eggs were on the menu.

They were similar types of men as the others, not quite so coarse perhaps. The bad language was something we had to accept and just hope that Vivienne wouldn't copy them. Their appetites were voracious; whatever I cooked was devoured in record time. My enormous stock pot bubbled daily on the stove, filled with home-made soup, often with suet dumplings. It made a good standby for lunch times, followed by cold mutton and salad. How tired we grew of this meat as the weeks passed, and longed for a joint of pork or beef. Shearing is a strange profession. According to all the Australians we met in the bush, their opinion of shearers was very low. They were described as 'the bottom of the heap' or the 'riff raff' and so on. A good shearer could work eleven months of the year, moving from state to state, as each state seemed to shear at different times. December was their holiday month, as it was for all workers, being mid-summer. This was the one period they could spend any length of time with their families.

Perhaps it was this nomadic existence that resulted in their rough manners, sleeping in a bunk house, doing their own laundry, eating in some farm kitchen or, on a really big station, bringing their own cook and setting up a mess room. It wasn't much of a life for them, I thought.

They negotiated their own rates of pay, so much per hundred sheep sheared and the farmers were careful to keep on the right side of the teams; one upset and they would down shears and move on to another farmer, who might pay more. The billycan routine began again, the endless trips to the sheds, the continual baking of cakes, pies and buns, in an effort to keep up with their appetites. The battle against the blowflies continued unabated and sometimes Vivienne would have to stand guard over the racks of baking while it cooled to prevent the flies from peppering it with maggots, waving a folded paper like a fan, just like the little coloured boys did in India when the Memsahib was resting. Mondays were the days I dreaded the most. The shearers would head for town as soon as they were free on Friday nights, and would return late at night in their truck, crates of beer stacked in the back. The weekends were spent drinking. If they were too drunk to come across for their meals they went without. I certainly didn't bother to call them. The sight of drunken men reeling about in my kitchen sickened me. There had never been any problem with Len or Wolf as neither of them were hard drinkers.

By Monday morning the team would be so 'hung over' that they could hardly see what they were doing. They would have the shakes and the effect on the poor sheep was horrific. Every ewe that staggered down the ramps, newly shorn, would be bleeding from a number of cuts. Some were so deep that their bones showed through, and were an immediate target for the flies, and in a few moments were crawling with maggots. Each shearer had a needle and coarse thread hanging by their implements, ready to sew up the cuts. This was done so roughly that I couldn't bear to watch. They would then dab on some orange liquid which made the poor beasts leap high in the air. Whatever sort of antiseptic it was, it must have stung them severely. Time was money to the shearers; they had no time to waste on a cut sheep.

A tremendous rivalry existed in the sheds, each man hoping to be the 'ringer' as the fastest shearer was called. A good 'ringer' could shear a hundred ewes in a day. The fleeces were collected from the floor as each ewe was finished and 'thrown' by Len or Roy Price in a skilled movement, so that it fell in a certain way on to a large table. It would then be graded by Mr Price or Edward and, according to quality, placed in huge piles ready to be baled by Ron and Wolf. It was hot, dusty work and the smell of sheep, sweat and dung was overpowering in the shed. To this day, if I walk round a country market where sheep are being sold, one whiff of that smell conjures up an image so clear that it might have happened only yesterday.

Every two hours an alarm clock would ring, by which time I would be waiting with the cans of tea to slake their thirst, and slabs of cake to keep them going until the next meal. After all the sheep had been shorn it was the turn of the lambs. They were then separated from their mothers and put into other paddocks. The noise was unbelievable as the mothers and babies tried to find each other again. It went on for days and was so distressing to hear, but like the cattle they gradually accepted their loss. The adult sheep were then dipped before being turned out to pasture again. I thought this a barbaric practice but it was law and had to be followed, just as it is in this country. A deep channel was filled with liquid, a ramp constructed at either end, down which the nervous creatures were pushed, prodded by a long pole with a crook at one end. They were held under for a full minute and came up struggling and spluttering, needing no more prodding to get up the ramp and away.

I understand that now a chemical has been perfected which is simply sprayed along their backbones and has the same effect as the dip. For once I say, hurrah for modern science!

I was having a lot of trouble at this time with the mail man who also brought our stores. He would frequently leave my goods elsewhere, he could never remember where exactly, but somehow I never got the benefit of the other people's goods. He wouldn't go back and look for them and we just had to manage until he came the next time.

One Friday when, yet again, he had lost my goods I let my temper get the better of me. 'How is it,' I raged, 'that you never seem to lose Wilma's or Mrs Price's things, why is it always mine?'

He scratched his head, wiped his nose on his sleeve as was his usual habit and said, 'Well, I brought your bread didn't I?' He held out the half dozen large loaves, unwrapped, and I turned them over, one by one.

'Look at them, look at this!' Bits of string, cigarette ends, pieces of coke and ash and heaven knows what else coated the bases. 'What do you do with these, do you use the sweepings of the bake house floor in your bread mixture?'

Every week I had to cut the bottoms off the bread. I dreaded to think what his bakehouse looked like. He just grinned, sniffed and said in his drawl, 'Guess you're a might too fussy, missus. My old woman, she don't care. If we can't eat it she just chucks it away,' and he slouched back to his truck, not one whit discomfited. I regretted the fact that we were not allowed to make our own bread. For some unknown reason it was illegal to buy yeast at that time and although I tried to start my own 'yeast plant' out of potato, which I had been told was possible, it never worked. So all the time I was there I had to endure Alf's dirty bread.

When Ron came in that night it was dark. He had just killed the daily sheep and hung it in the stone outhouse. By morning it was such a seething mass of maggots that I despaired of cleaning up in time to cook it for the evening meal.

I had ordered some beef to break the monotony of mutton but I guess that was being enjoyed at some other table by now. The shearers had departed to start their shift and I said, 'Take the gun, Ron, see if you can get a rabbit, anything for a change.' He picked up the rifle and I handed him the magazine with its ten bullets, which I always carried in my trouser pocket for safety; we never left the gun loaded. He walked out of the door, I heard one shot and he walked back in, handing me the largest rabbit I have ever seen. I took it and said, stupidly, 'Wherever did you get it?'

With a wink he said, 'A man just happened to be passing by and asked me if I would like a nice rabbit.'

We both laughed; what a stroke of luck for us that the poor animal just hopped by at that moment! I made it into an enormous stew which even the shearers enjoyed, as I heard one of them say to Ron that evening, 'Hey, your old lady don't cook at all bad.' Praise indeed.

When the shearing was finally over Wolf decided he would leave and travel across to the eastern states, as he felt he wanted to see more of the country. He worked out his month's notice and left for Queensland. We knew as little about him when he left as we had the first day we had met him. We never saw or heard of him again.

One letter came from Bill and Sally. Things weren't working out very well for them. Having had no success in finding a joint position, Bill had taken a living-in job in a country hotel, while Sally started as a domestic help in a big mental hospital. She shared a room with another girl, but was not happy in the job and, of course, missing her husband. She found it hard to write in English and had given us no address to reply to. I felt sorry for them and wondered if they would be able to save the fare back to Holland.

Edward and Wilma packed up their belongings to return to their home in Perth, taking Len with them for a couple of weeks holiday. The Prices also went down to the city, to their town house, with Roy, leaving Ron, Vivienne and me alone on the farm. How empty it all seemed, all those miles and no one around but us. Mr Price had left a detailed list of all the jobs he wanted done by the time he returned so Ron was absent all day, miles away usually, fencing in some distant paddock.

Vivienne continued with her lessons, somewhat neglected during the shearing, and I taught myself to play the piano accordion from the Dutch box. I am not particularly musical but I mastered 'Land of Hope and Glory', 'Sussex by the Sea', and one or two of the popular tunes of the day. It was a dreadfully lonely time and I wrote countless letters to family and friends at home, when the mail man remembered to take them. I think he must have been amazed at the number he had to take to post each time he came. I even found myself looking forward to his visits, sheer desperation! Ron didn't look forward to the visits very much; he knew that if there hadn't been any mail from home, he would be in for a bleak weekend! He would pause and listen before he came in after milking and if he heard 'Sussex by the Sea' drifting across the sand he knew it would be doom and gloom until the next mail call.

During the days I was somewhat nervous, for we had no locks on the doors and had been warned that after the shearing, groups of rough characters would go round the farms trying to buy cheaply any dead wool left over. They were usually halfcastes, belonging to neither one race or the other, making a few pounds wherever they could. The equivalent of our tinkers, I suppose. When Ron used to leave in the mornings I would say, 'Leave me the gun today, I feel safer if I have it near me.' He liked to take it sometimes in case he saw a rabbit to supplement our diet.

'Well be careful with it, don't leave it loaded and if anyone does come round, stay indoors.'

He need not have reminded me. I was very careful with it; guns are too dangerous to be treated lightly. Whether I would have had the nerve to shoot I don't know; thank goodness I never had the occasion to find out. We only had one scare, a very hot day when the door and windows were all open. We heard a truck coming down the track and the familiar barking of the dog. I hastily shut the windows and door and heard the truck screech to a halt at the other cottage. Several men climbed out and we could hear them hammering on the door. I slid the magazine into the rifle, called Vivienne to come with me and we crouched on the floor under the bedroom window. This was the one window which would be most difficult to look into. We heard them come to our door, bang on it and walk round the house, bang on the front window, and the sound of their voices, before they moved away. They drove across to the main house and, having no answer anywhere, climbed into their truck and roared off up the track again.

They were probably quite harmless but I felt so vulnerable that I wasn't taking any chances. Screams would have been useless with no one for miles around to hear. I was quite relieved when the Prices returned, bringing Len back with them. There are times when any company is better than none!

Chapter 16

Return to Town

The weather was growing hotter and the wheat grew with it. Thankfully, the blowflies began to disappear but another pest came to haunt me. Strictly speaking, moths are not a pest but I am terrified of them, and these were no ordinary moths! If there had been a shower of rain or a heavy dew the ground in the early morning would be littered with large larva cases. The first time I saw them I couldn't think what they were: brown skins, like a finger stall, each one lying beside a hole in the ground. In the evening I knew what they were! It was already dark and Ron would soon be in for his meal and I had been across to the privy. As I neared the house I saw what looked like a bat, clinging to the fly wires over the door and kitchen window. Not one, I realised, but a dozen or more, as, with horror, I watched them fling themselves against the wire trying to get inside. They were enormous moths, as big as an English sparrow, with furry bodies almost the size of my fist. I was too scared to open the door, lest the creatures should get into the house, and I hovered anxiously outside until Ron arrived. All evening they were banging against the wires, attracted by the lights, no doubt, flying away when the house was in darkness after we had gone to bed. By early morning the butcher birds, with their wicked beaks, were feasting on the bodies. It was probably a real delicacy for them. The season for the moths was quickly over. It was amazing that any remained to reproduce their species in view of the attentions of the butcher birds.

During October we began to think about sending home a Christmas parcel and Ron suggested that I should go down to Perth for a few days and do some shopping. A train ran twice a week and there was a halt at Binnie

where I could board it so Ron asked Mr Price if he could have an afternoon
off, borrow the small truck and take Vivienne and me to catch the train. To
our surprise he said that if I could wait a few days he and Mrs Price were
going down to the 'Royal Show', which was an annual event. Anybody who
was anybody in the farming world went to the show, many of them of
course exhibiting cattle or sheep. Indeed, the entire population of that part
of Australia flocked to the city for the whole week. Len and Roy were also
going which would leave Ron entirely alone, but he didn't mind. Roy had a
car of his own and Len went with him; Vivienne and I were to follow with
the Prices in their huge American Cadillac. I had ridden in this car twice
previously and been terribly carsick each time. I wondered how I would fare
for hundreds of miles when I couldn't get to Binnie and back without
throwing up! It was true that on the previous occasions I had only been to
the store while Mrs Price had been visiting friends and she was a very erratic
driver; perhaps with Mr Price at the wheel and good roads for most of the
way it might be better. Anyway the chance of a free lift was too good to
turn down. We set off in the late morning, Vivienne and I sitting in the back
with one suitcase between us. It was such a well-sprung car that it swayed a
great deal and I felt very ill, but I was determined not to disgrace myself and
practised deep breathing and reached Perth safely. We had two breaks on
the way for refreshment which gave me a short time to recover and it was
almost dusk as we entered the city.

The Price's town house was beautiful, brick-built and two storied, which
was unusual. She showed me round, proudly; her town house was obviously
a delight to her. The bedroom was vast, wardrobes ranged the length of one
wall. She slid the doors aside and I gasped. I have never seen so many
clothes in my life! Dresses, suits, coats and skirts by the score, and on racks
at the bottom enough shoes and sandals to stock a shoe shop! The house
itself had every luxury imaginable and I thought perhaps that was what
made her one of the most discontented people I have ever met. I thought of
all that opulence down in the city for her occasional use while most of her
days were spent in the bush!

We ate a light meal there, then she said, 'Where are you going to
stay?'

I replied, 'I'll find a room in a guest house somewhere for a few days.'
There was no mention of my return to the farm but I knew they were
intending to stay a fortnight, so I would go back by train at the weekend.

'George will drop you back in the city, then.' she said. 'You'd better get
going, we'll see you back at Korrine.'

I thanked her for the meal and the lift. I felt as if she and I were as near to being friendly as we ever would be. Mr Price set us down in one of the main streets where there were a number of small guest houses and hotels and drove away. Vivienne and I walked along, with me carrying the case, which grew heavier with every step, and began to call at the various establishments. It was dark, of course and what I hadn't expected was to find everywhere full. I should have realised that with the Royal Show on, the city would be teeming with people. I got the same answer in so many places, 'Sorry, we are fully booked for the whole week; it's the Show, you know.' By ten o'clock I was getting desperate and Vivienne was tired and dragging behind me. I could see us ending up on a park bench!

Finally I ended up at the Grand Hotel, one of the plushiest in the city. They had one double room owing to a cancellation, for two nights only. It was much too expensive, really, but I took it hoping I could find somewhere else during the next two days. We were shown to our room by a very polite young porter, who told us that breakfast was served from eight a.m. until nine thirty, and we washed the dust from our hands and faces before tumbling thankfully into bed.

We had a leisurely bath in the morning. What bliss, to lie and soak in clean scented water in a sumptuous bathroom, a far cry from the rusty water and chip heater of Korrine. We dressed and went down to the dining room. Talk about the proverbial country cousins! I was wearing a skirt and jumper with heavy walking shoes, the sort we always wore on the farm. In fact, I had very few clothes, and after seven months of living in jeans and shirts I had completely forgotten what folk would be wearing in town. As we entered the dining room I looked at the tables set for four, dotted around on what seemed acres of carpet, the waitresses dressed in formal black and white attending the guests, and felt utterly out of place. A hostess, as she was called, glided across the room toward us, elegant in her silk suit and spiky-heeled shoes, her blonded hair carefully coiffured, and held out her hand to shake mine, her blood-red nails as long as talons.

She held a clipboard to which she referred and asked my room number. 'Mrs and Miss Upton,' she gushed, 'Welcome to you both. Let me show you to your table.' She turned, a whiff of expensive perfume enveloping her, and we followed her to a table near one of the big windows. An elderly couple were sitting there. 'Let me introduce you to Mr and Mrs James Brewster; you may know each other. No doubt you are all down for the Show.' I have often thought about this incident. It was probably the normal procedure in hotels of this class, and it was assumed that anyone staying during the Show week would know each other. Maybe she thought I was an eccentric wife of some wealthy farmer! How little she knew!

Mr and Mrs Brewster were pleasant but as they had almost finished their meal we had no real conversation. A waitress appeared and handed me the menu. I chose my breakfast and she took the menu from me. 'And what will the little girl have?' she asked.

I replied, 'You may let her choose for herself.'

I thought for the money we were paying we could certainly eat what we liked. Surprised, she handed the ornate card to Vivienne. She read it for a moment or two.

'Fruit juice, then a fried egg and two pork sausages, large ones please,' she said and handed the menu back. At that age she did not realise that sausages were really meat. The waitress's face was a picture.

'Will she actually eat it, madam?' she asked, 'And did she really read it?'

'Certainly she read it, and she will eat it, thank you,' I replied.

She went away and the Brewsters, who were about to leave the table, were highly amused. I felt so embarrassed and thought to myself that she would eat it, even if we sat there for an hour!

We thoroughly enjoyed the morning, shopping in town. There are some lovely stores in Perth and we found all sorts of little novelties to send home. They had to be fairly small presents or the postage would be too high, but we ended up with a delightful selection. Needless to say we did not lunch at the hotel; the bill would be quite high enough for the bed and breakfast! In the afternoon we caught a train to Tinton and called on some of our old neighbours. It was nice to see them again, especially May and Alan. We had a meal with them about six o'clock and May suggested that, although she had no room in the house to sleep us, we could sleep on her verandah. Most people slept out during the hot weather and May, like others, had several small iron bedsteads for this purpose. I was grateful for this opportunity as I knew I would have difficulty in finding cheap accommodation in the overcrowded city. We returned to the hotel for the night promising to be back to May in time for lunch the next day.

I had asked Ron to send a letter to me, care of May as I didn't know where I would be staying, and a day or so later a letter duly arrived. He said how lonely it was, no one else for miles, keeping an eye on the sheep, the cows, hens and dogs. Mr Price had, as before, left a list of jobs to be done while he was away. One of these was to remove the large stones from some of the dried-up wells. The artesian bores with their metal windmills were dotted around the land, drawing up water for the animals. It was mineral water, slightly salty, and unsuitable for human consumption. The wells were like small ponds some twenty feet across with sloping sides, the centre being as much as sixty feet where the water went into the ground. Stones were hard to come by up in the bush and those that lined the upper part of the wells had to be removed when the water dried up, then used to line another well. Mr Price had his own drilling rig and a new bore would be sunk, hopefully finding more water, a well dug, and a windmill erected.

Ron wrote that he had been down a dry well, removing stones and had just prised out a huge rock when a snake darted out from the hole, disturbed of course, from its sleep, and tried to bite his face. He hit it with the crowbar he was holding and killed it. Immediately its mate emerged from the same hole and attacked him. He was fortunate in jumping aside in time, but several other near misses down the same well convinced him that the stones could wait until he had a working companion. I read the letter out to May.

'I'm really worried about the snakes,' I said. 'We have no phone up there and no vehicle of our own; it's my biggest fear that Vivienne will be bitten one day and whatever could I do? By the time we could get to a doctor it would be too late. I have nightmares about it.'

I did, frequently, and would wake shaking with terror. Another letter arrived some days later, although he had not yet received one from me. In this one he told me that he had discovered several snakes' nests in and around the garden. My mind was made up. I did not want to return to Binnie, and only two days later I picked up May's daily paper to read of the death of a six-year-old boy not many miles from Korrine. His mother had gone into his bedroom and found two small puncture marks on his ankle. He was already in a coma and before they could get him to the nearest hospital he had died. NO, we would not go back to Korrine, that was certain. I sent a letter straight off to Ron, asking him to phone me at May's on the Saturday, hoping it would arrive in time to be taken out to the farm on the Friday mail run.

With no one on the farm I knew he could borrow the small truck, drive into Binnie, and phone me from the saloon. I was delighted when the phone rang at about eight-thirty on Saturday and May confirmed it was Ron on the line. It was almost two weeks since we had left Korrine but I didn't want to waste time on unnecessary conversation. Business first.

'We're fine and enjoying the break. I've had two letters from you and I'm very worried about the snake situation.' I poured out my fears. 'I don't want to come back. There seems to be much more work about now, in the city. If I can find a cheap furnished room, would you come and join us? I know it means giving a month's notice but Vivienne and I will be OK. Then when it is time for you to come down, I could arrange for a truck to come and fetch you.'

He didn't sound in the least surprised; in some ways I think it was almost a relief to him. 'I think I knew, the moment you had driven away, that you wouldn't be back. It's all right, you find a room, then let me know. The Prices should be back in about four days, but I won't give my notice in until I hear from you. Take care of yourselves, I'll just have a few words with Vivienne, can't say much as I haven't got any more change and someone is waiting to use the box.'

He said hullo to Vivienne before having to ring off. What a relief: no more snakes or flies, no more isolation, I would find a really nice room in Perth and Vivienne and I could move in and make it homely before he arrived. I told May and Alan of our plans and May, ever practical, said 'How are you going to manage for money?'

I said, 'I've got the cheque book, I left Ron enough cash to last for a couple of weeks, then he can live on the store boxes. After all, there will only be him to eat the food. If Len does go back with Roy Price he will have to eat with them. They couldn't expect Ron to cook for Len.'

Late that night as I lay on the verandah, listening to the strange noises of the night, I felt quite excited. On Monday morning I would leave Vivienne with May and go into Perth, call on some agencies and view some rooms. I felt sure I would find one easily. It wouldn't be for many months as next year we were going home. Perth was, and still is, I'm sure, a lovely city, with some beautiful parks and shops. I could settle happily there until we sailed. Vivienne would be able to go to a proper school, I might even be able to get myself a part-time job, and save some money to help with the fares home. My head full of plans, I fell asleep.

Chapter 17

New Street

I left Vivienne with May on the Monday and caught the train into Perth to start my search. There were several agencies that dealt only in furnished flats and rooms and I had made a list of these. One by one I visited them, becoming more and more despondent. The prices of the flats were well beyond our reach but I had thought that there would be plenty of choice in flatlets. There were a few but they were so far out of the city that they were impractical. I had to consider Ron's fares to work if he got a job in the centre of town and a school for Vivienne. By lunch time I had looked at several rooms, which were so awful that I wouldn't consider them, and three others that were already under offer. One lady took my name but said it was most unlikely that her prospective lodger wouldn't return with the deposit by teatime.

I ate a sandwich at a snack bar and continued visiting the agencies. At four o'clock I had exhausted my list, and was about to go back to the station and return to Tinton, when I saw a board in a shop window filled with cards. There at the top was a printed notice, 'To let. Furnished room and small kitchen. Apply 91 New Street between four and five p.m.' I entered the shop and asked for directions to New Street and found it was a ten minute walk away. My hopes rose; I could make it before five. I still had to ask a passer-by for more directions, for after I had crossed a large bridge I must have taken a wrong turning so it was almost the five o'clock deadline when I found the house. The street was long and very shabby, the usual timber and asbestos bungalows with iron roofs and verandahs running along the fronts. Number ninety-one had a wire fence with a rusty gate and a patch of sand for a front garden. The door stood wide open. I knocked, and after a moment a woman appeared. She was short and plump with black hair pulled back into a bun and dark brown eyes. I thought she was Italian but when she spoke she had a strong Irish accent.

'What can I do for you?' she asked.

'I saw an advert in a shop window about a room to let,' I began, but got no further. With a cry she flung her arms around me and burst into tears.

'Oh, you're from home, someone from home,' she sobbed. 'Come in, come in.'

Somewhat taken aback I followed her inside, and went into a small room with no window and a sink in one corner.

'Sit down, please. Oh, I can't tell you how pleased I am to see someone from home, I hate this life, hate it,' with great emphasis on the last phrase. 'We're saving up to go home, what about you?'

She poured out her story, and whatever had possessed the O'Malleys (for that was their name) to emigrate I shall never know. They were in their fifties and had left three married daughters and a son in England, bringing the youngest four children with them. Nothing had gone right for them since they had arrived; how often had I heard this story. Her husband had at last found work as a factory cleaner and she herself worked in a number of places, mainly cleaning and washing. There were twins of nine, Kenny and Kim, and a thirteen-year-old girl, Sara. Peter was sixteen and was still trying to find employment.

They occupied the front room, which was used as a bed-sitting room, a smaller room behind it and the tiny dark kitchen, where we now sat. How they sorted out the sleeping arrangements was, and remained, a mystery. The passage ran through the middle of the house with three rooms each side, so the O'Malleys had the whole of one side. On the other side of the passage the front room was let to a young couple called Les and Mary Thorne. They were both from the Midlands and had been sent to Australia when quite young, under a scheme run by a charity. They had lost touch with their families. We know now that, at the outbreak of war, a large number of children were shipped out to the country, from poor areas of England, placed in these farm schools and never encouraged to write to their families. It has been discovered since that this was a deliberate policy, a way of gaining cheap labour for the farms. The boys were all trained in farm work and the girls put into domestic service.

It has only lately been highlighted again and an organisation now exists to try to find some of the families and put them in touch with their long-lost children. At that time Mary and Les knew nothing of this, but were bitter that probably somewhere in England they had brothers and sisters, and perhaps parents still living. They were newly married and worked as shop assistants in the city.

Mrs O'Malley certainly knew the backgrounds of the inhabitants of the house. The back room was let to a widow, also English, who had lived in the Far East all her married life. She had been in Singapore when it fell to the Japanese and had spent almost four years in a prison camp. Her husband and son had been in another camp, and after the war when she was finally free she was reunited with her now teenage son, but learned that her husband had not survived the ordeal. She had settled in Australia as she had no relations in England, and lived very frugally on a small pension. She was in poor health as a result of her years in captivity and rarely went out. Sometimes she used to talk of her dreadful years, and I often wondered if the victims of those camps should have had more compensation.

The middle room was the one to let, and Mrs O'Malley ushered me inside. It was so dark that she had to switch the light on and I realised why. The one small window looked out directly onto the wall of the house next door. The floor was covered in brown lino and the room was sparsely furnished with one wardrobe, a double bed, a chest of drawers, a small table and two chairs. I did a quick calculation. We had our camp table and chairs and the folding bed, which there would be room for; the rent was cheap, less than four pounds a week; I would take it.

'I think a kitchen was mentioned, could you show me?' I asked.

We went outside the back door where there was a lean-to. It had been partitioned off and one section contained a food cupboard, a bench and table and a two-burner cooker. This was included in the rent. There was no sink or tap but a standpipe outside was available, to be shared by us all. The other piece of the lean-to had been converted into a makeshift bathroom with a cracked basin, a shower and a gas meter. A couple of coppers put into the meter gave enough hot water for a shower and the entire occupants of the house shared this room. The toilet was at the end of the back garden but at least it had a flush cistern, something of a luxury for us now!

'Please say you'll take it,' Mrs O'Malley begged. 'Mrs Tanner and the Thornes are pleasant, but they aren't really English any more.' She obviously didn't consider that being Irish herself I might not consider her English either!

'Yes, I'll take it, but I shall want to clean it up a bit first. Who owns it, or who do I pay the rent to?'

'We don't know who owns it, someone on behalf of the owner collects the rent every two weeks but nothing is ever done in the way of repairs or decoration, as you can see for yourself. We take it in turns to clean the passage and the bathroom.'

I explained that Ron wouldn't be down for a month but that Vivienne and I would move in quite soon. We could manage well enough with the bedding and kitchen utensils that were already there until Ron arrived with our belongings. I returned to May quite pleased that I had found somewhere. Next day I bought a large can of whitewash and a brush and went to New Street to give my new home a face lift. I thought the white walls would make the dark room look a bit lighter and it certainly needed a clean up anyway. Being only five feet tall and having no step-ladder was a problem as it meant I could only do the walls as far as I could reach from a chair, and not touch the ceiling at all, but it looked and smelled fresh and clean when finished. We moved in three days later, having written to Ron giving him our new address. I asked him to let me know the actual day he would be leaving the farm so that I could arrange for a truck to go and fetch him. I decided it wouldn't be fair to ask Alan again.

After the first few days in our new abode I realised that hardly anybody around us spoke English. All the shops nearby were owned by Greeks or Chinese and the people on the streets spoke in every foreign language imaginable. I asked Mrs O'Malley one day why this was. 'Is there any reason why I never seem to hear English spoken?'

'Bless you, yes. This is the foreign quarter, more or less. To be honest, it's just the dregs round here. They say only foreigners and no hopers live in these parts; anyone who has any money lives over the bridge.'

She gave a wink and a nod as if I should know exactly what she meant. I soon did! One night I woke up to hear a movement at the door, which had no lock. Vivienne was fast asleep and Ron still up at Korrine. I switched on the light and saw the door handle being gently turned.

'Who's there?' I asked sharply, getting out of bed.

A grunt answered me but by the time I got across to the door and flung it wide the visitor was disappearing through the front door. I waylaid Mary Thorne in the morning as she left for work.

'Tell me something, Mary, what is it about this area that is strange? I've only been here a week but, apart from the fact that it is the foreign quarter, why are there so many men about? I see very few women compared with the number of men.'

She chuckled. 'Didn't they tell you, this is the red light district! The brothels are only just round the corner; most of the houses here are lodging houses, full of single men, mostly Greek or Italian, that's why you see all men.'

I told her about the night visitor. She wasn't surprised.

'He was just looking for a woman, I expect. Pity we have no locks for any of the doors. We've put a bolt on the inside of our room; you want to get your old man to do the same when he comes. Stick a chair under the handle until then, then you'll be OK.'

She didn't seem unduly perturbed and I must admit that I soon got used to sleeping with a chair propped under the handle, and felt quite safe.

I wrote home telling the family all about our new area, omitting any mention of the brothels. We had a letter from Phillip and Joy every few weeks. They had rented a piece of land with a small dwelling on it and started a market garden. They seemed very happy, as did Hans and Corrie who also wrote regularly. They were staying with Corrie's mother but had managed to buy a plot of land on which Hans was going to build a bungalow, as and when they could save enough money to start. I longed for the time when I could write to them and say we were on our way home.

Vivienne and I soon slipped into a routine. I found a school for her, about fifteen minutes walk away. The junior school that the O'Malley children went to was for children over eight years old so was no use for Vivienne but, although the school I found was a Catholic one they didn't object to non-Catholic pupils. It was called St. Bridget's and was an old grey stone building, adjoining a large church. I realised just how many foreign people there must be in the district, for almost every hour of the day a Mass was held, each time in a different language.

By the time Ron was due from Korrine it was almost December and we were well settled in New Street. Vivienne loved the school. Her teacher was Sister Mary Theresa, a gentle Irish nun with such a sense of humour, but a dedicated teacher. She needed to be, for out of forty-five children in her class there were only three who spoke English as their mother tongue: Vivienne and two classmates, Yolande and Shane, who were both Australian. The rest of the class were from Latvia, Poland, Greece, Hungary, Bulgaria, Italy, the Ukraine, Germany, Holland, Yugoslavia and others I can't remember. I know we once counted fourteen different nationalities among her school friends.

Sister Mary Theresa for all her gentle manner was very strict with the children. She told me once that if she hadn't taught the rudiments of reading to each child in her class at the end of their first term, even though English was not their normal language, she felt she had failed. The one disadvantage of her 'by rote' method was that Vivienne read everything now in a broad Irish accent!

The weather by the end of November was extremely hot and our room almost unbearable. Being so close to the wall of the house next door we had no fresh air at all and the light had to be on all day. I always took Vivienne to school and fetched her as there were three busy roads to cross, so I had a good walk each day and the chance to get out in the sun. Just before we got to the school itself we had to cross a small park. This was the part I dreaded. Invariably there were drunken men, sprawling about the grass. It was a haunt for the winos and drug addicts of the district and even at eight-thirty in the morning they would be fighting mad. Some days they would be attacking each other with cut-throat razors. I thought about Mrs O'Malley's remarks about this area being for foreigners and no-hopers; well, these poor wretches were certainly no-hopers, and I wondered which category we came in!

Each day as I met Vivienne from school these men would be filing into the Convent grounds to receive a slice of bread and a bowl of soup, provided by the nuns. One afternoon I said to Sister Mary Theresa, 'Isn't it awful, these down and out people and the conditions in the streets around here, the brothels and so on?'

She smiled sweetly. 'We are all God's creatures, Mrs Upton, no matter what we do, but you know,' and here her eyes twinkled merrily, 'Every time I cross the park and see the degradation around me, I thank God I'm a nun!' Cloistered as they were at times there was no doubt that the nuns of St. Bridget's knew the ways of the world.

Ron was due to arrive on a Saturday evening. I had arranged for a truck to go and fetch him, after seeing a telephone number to ring in the daily paper. My conversation with the driver had been brief, just the details of where to go and who to ask for, payment to be made on arrival. When Ron arrived later in the evening we had hardly greeted each other before he said, 'You can't stay here!'

'What do you mean, we can't stay here?'

He stared at me then said, 'Don't you realise, you are living in the middle of the red light area?'

'Yes, I know now. I had no idea when I took the room, though. It's not too bad, the room is cheap, Vivienne likes her school and it is close to the city centre ready for when you get a job. Don't you think we have moved around enough? I don't want to move again until we leave for home.'

He was adamant. 'I can't let you and Vivienne stay here, the lorry driver told me what sort of a place it is. It wouldn't be right.' Then he explained what had happened. He was still working at Korrine when the truck arrived, Mr Price had insisted that a piece of fencing was completed before he was allowed to leave. All our belongings had been packed the night before and Ron hadn't bothered to light the stove as he wasn't sure what time the truck would come. So the poor driver, having driven all that way wasn't even able to have a drink. It didn't occur to the Prices to offer any refreshment so Ron had a quick wash in the laundry trough as soon as he had finished the fence, said his goodbyes to the Prices, received his cheque up to date and loaded the truck. As soon as they had reached Binnie they had gone to the saloon where Ron bought such food as they had to offer.

There wasn't much conversation on the journey. The driver was a man of few words and Ron was weary and glad to sit back and be driven. As they neared Perth the driver said, 'What address am I taking you to? Your wife only spoke to me on the phone, she just said to bring you to town.'

Ron answered, 'Ninety-one New Street.'

There was a silence, then, 'Would you say that again, mate?'

He repeated the address. The truck stopped and the driver turned to face him.

'I think you've made a mistake, sport, that's over the Horseshore Bridge.'

'What do you mean, over the Horseshoe Bridge? That's the address I've been sending letters to.'

'It's the red light area, no one decent lives there, they're all dings and dagos, hookers and no-hopers there. Your wife wouldn't take a room in such a place surely?'

Ron was horrified and agreed that if it were indeed as bad as he had been told then the quicker he got us out of there, the better. Hence his dismay on arrival to hear that we really were in the middle of the brothel area. We sat up for hours and talked it over. I tried to explain that we could keep ourselves to ourselves, that it wouldn't be for very long and just think, if he could get a job in the city itself, look at the money we could save!

'Give it a week or two,' I pleaded, 'See where you get work. Remember, rooms are hard to come by and this is cheap, that's the most important thing. The less we spend, the more we can save for our fares.'

Finally, he was persuaded, we would stay. New Street would be our last address in Australia!

Chapter 18

City Life

Ron was very lucky to find a job within a few days, just a temporary one. His experience at the oat mill at Tinton stood him in good stead, for he was taken on as a miller in a flour mill. The hours were unsocial, two-thirty until eleven p.m. every weekday, but the wages were good. Going to work was a source of amusement to him, for he had to walk down the notorious Roe Street *en route*. This was the heart of the brothel trade, a row of small bungalows with wire fronted, cage-like verandahs, where the girls sat advertising their wares. In the afternoons most of the prostitutes were older women, who would call out their prices quite openly, trying to entice the male passersby inside. After eleven o'clock, when he walked home, the girls were much younger, some of them really beautiful, and didn't need to solicit the men, for there was always a steady flow of clients. Roe Street also contained the girls' Grammer School and the main Police Station! While the brothels weren't exactly legal they were tolerated, and if there was the slightest trouble the girls would call the police without hesitation.

They were all medically examined each week and the whole business was well run. During the months that we lived in New Street there was a campaign mounted by the churches to have them all closed. This caused such an outcry that the idea was dropped, the consensus of public opinion being that, in a country with such an overwhelming number of single men, it was a necessary service. We certainly agreed; as it was, it was impossible to walk the streets alone in the evenings if you were a woman without being accosted continually and asked your price. Ron had put a secure bolt on our room door soon after he arrived, but we still had 'night visitors', trying the handle, and sometimes in the mornings we would find a drunk lying under the verandah.

It seemed that any house in that district was assumed to be a brothel and that any young woman alone was 'on the game'. I understand that Roe Street is no longer operating and the establishments today are palatial houses in nice suburbs, still not legal, but 'controlled' as the police put it, with a 'madam' firmly in charge.

Not long before Christmas, Derek Greenfield sailed for home; he would just arrive in time for the New Year festivities. Maureen had given birth to a little girl several months previously but Derek had only just managed to sell his plot and dwelling. He was excited to be going home for he had been very lonely since Maureen's departure, living in his bare little garage and not daring to spend a penny more than was necessary. He had been to visit us a number of times and could never conceal his astonishment that we were living in such seedy surroundings.

Of course, we were going down to the docks to say our goodbyes. I lost count of the times we went to Fremantle to see friends off; it seemed that every week we knew someone going home. Derek was sailing on the *Oronsay*, a large ship of the Orient Line. We went aboard to see his cabin and spent the last half hour with him. When they called 'All visitors ashore' we went down the gangplank to the strains of 'Now is the Hour' and mingled with the throng on the quay. There was a delay before the ship sailed and the band continued to play, a selection of lively tunes. They struck up 'Sussex by the Sea' and I was near to tears, then a voice in the crowd shouted out, 'Play one for me, "Maybe it's because I'm a Londoner".'

The voice sounded familiar and I pushed my way through the crowd. There stood Jean Mills, holding a child of about a year old, her husband Frank and the other three children clustering round her. Tears poured down her cheeks, but she and the family were all singing heartily. What emotional occasions these sailings were. We hugged each other, unable to speak, as the streamers were thrown and the *Oronsay* steamed slowly away. We had not seen each other since the journey out and there was so much to catch up on. Frank had purchased an old car into which we all piled, and they took us back to their room in Fremantle.

They had one large room where they lived and slept and, like us in New Street, a portion of the lean-to for a kitchen. The room was much bigger than ours. It needed to be for James was almost sixteen and about to leave school, Janet and Lillian were seven and five and the baby, Colin, fourteen months old. We had a meal with them and how we talked! Jean was not in the best of health as Colin's birth had been a difficult one and afterwards she had contracted one illness after another. There was no health service at that time; you had to pay in for private care, but of course there was a qualifying period. Jean, being pregnant when she arrived, did not qualify and their savings from the sale of their house in London had been almost swallowed up in doctor's bills. The sister with whom they had at first stayed had sailed for home within a few months of Jean and Frank's arrival, selling their house, and leaving the Mills family homeless. I had seen this happen so many times during my time in Australia and still can't understand why anyone who had booked a passage home did not tell their relations the truth. Perhaps they felt that if some of their family came out to join them it would help them, themselves, to settle down. The Mills family had only been able to afford this room in Fremantle, for although Frank was a qualified electrician he had been able to find employment just as an electrician's mate, owing to the usual Union ticket problem. They had already booked their passage home and were saving as hard as they could as their fares would cost about eight hundred pounds, a great deal of money. We did enjoy seeing them again, and thus began a close friendship that still continues.

Ron's job with the flour mill ended but again he was lucky. He was taken on as a scaffolder with a firm who were building a new hospital in the city. It was only for a few weeks as most of the firms closed down at Christmas, apart from the shops, it being the main summer holiday. We spent every Sunday with Frank and Jean and the children, although James considered he was now too old to go out with his parents. Just as well; their old banger could hardly carry the rest of us, four adults and four children! We would squeeze in somehow, plus picnic baskets, and go out into the country, the beach or one of the parks.

Friday nights we spent together, one week at their house, the next at ours. Frank always drove us back from our visits to them although we went down on the train. The journey back to New Street took us through Roe Street, which on a Friday night was an amazing sight. Being pay night, I suppose, it was one the busiest times. Queues of men would wait on the pavements, outside the brothel of their choice, eyeing the girls until they entered. The children were curious as to what was going on. One night Vivienne said, 'Daddy, why are all those men lined up looking at the girls in the cages?'

Ron replied, 'They are the dancing girls, the men are waiting to go in and see them dance.'

Years later, when she was about fourteen, we drove down a similar street in England, not a red light street, but similar in length and architecture. There was a railway at the end with a bridge over the road and Vivienne suddenly said, 'Doesn't this remind you of the street in Australia, where all the dancing girls were?' She had never mentioned that in all the years between, so we enlightened her as to the true profession of the girls. It made me realise what long memories small children can have; perhaps we underestimate them! The nights that Jean and Frank came to us we would eat in our tiny kitchen, then carry the bench and some chairs out onto the verandah, it being too hot to stay indoors.

On the corner of the street was a large saloon bar and immediately opposite our house a narrow street called Penny Road. A tall tree stood at the junction of New Street and Penny Road, a kind of willow, with drooping branches reaching to the ground. For some reason this tree had become a makeshift urinal for the half-drunk men who staggered down the pavement after the bar closed at nine o'clock. A number of these would push their way into the drooping branches to relieve themselves, all very unhygienic but funny to the onlookers. One Friday morning the council workmen came with saws and ladders and cut most of the branches away, leaving a tall bald tree, with a few leaves at the top. That night as we, with the Mills family and the O'Malleys, sat there, down came the revellers in their usual state, heading for their tree, only to find a bare trunk! I have never seen anything so funny as they milled around, pushing and shoving each other, shouting and swearing, wondering, no doubt, if they were in the right street! We laughed until the tears ran down our faces. Our entertainment was cheap, if somewhat earthy!

Ron's scaffolding job ended on Christmas Eve. The firm was closing for almost a month and the bosses provided kegs of beer and sandwiches, laid out in the cool concrete basement of the building. The iron scaffold poles were so hot during the day that the men had to wear heavy leather gloves or they would lose the skin from their hands. Underneath, in what was to be the car park, it was dark and cool. Several dozen Italian lads worked as labourers on the site, many of whom lived in the lodging houses in our area. A few of them had taken their accordions with them to have a sing-song at the end of the afternoon. The bosses stopped the workers at three o'clock and they all went down to where the refreshments were laid out on trestle tables. The atmosphere was very convivial and, after the food had been eaten and most of the beer drunk, the music started. The Italians, like most of their race, could sing well, and they played and sang carols and many of their own Neapolitan songs, ending with the emotional 'Mama'. Ron said it was one of the most moving hours he had ever sat through; there they were, these tough young men, singing their hearts out, tears streaming down their cheeks, as they sang of their beloved Italy!

We spent Christmas Day with May and Alan. They had a barbecue in their garden and we met all our old neighbours again. It was a much more cheerful day than Christmas the previous year had been. On Boxing Day we went to a National Park with Jean, Frank and the children; it was a lovely setting with cool streams and trees and was one of our favourite places. We had a special picnic, with cold Christmas pudding to finish our meal, and talked of what we would do the next Christmas. Jean said, 'What a celebration we shall have! All the family, roast turkey, nuts, a log fire, a tree and maybe even some snow!' With temperatures soaring over a hundred degrees it was a pleasing prospect.

As soon as the holiday was over and the business began to open again Ron answered an advert for a packer in a large electrical firm. They had a huge shop in the city centre where they sold fridges, washing machines, etc., to the general public, and a store where they supplied goods to the trade. He was given the job, and really enjoyed it, packing items for delivery all over the world. He also went out on the vans, sometimes driving the trucks and, if there were deliveries which required two men, he went with a giant of a man called Jimmy Bloom. Unfortunately, within three weeks of starting his new job he was taken ill.

There was a polio epidemic raging at the time, many new cases being reported each day. The children were on their long summer holiday and the house was so noisy with their games that I would take them out with me every day. Such a crowd of them it seemed, but anywhere away from the house so that Ron could have a little peace. Mr and Mrs O'Malley were at work all day so the children were left to their own devices. As the days wore on and Ron grew worse I sent for a doctor. The pains in Ron's head and limbs were almost unbearable; he couldn't even bear the sheet on him. The doctor said he was afraid it was polio but he did not want to move him, unless within a few days the actual paralysis set in. What a dreadful week that was, the airless room, the excessive heat and the fact that even a bottle of cold drink bought at the corner shop was warm by the time I reached the house. I had nothing to give him any relief. The medicines and tablets the doctor had prescribed were very expensive and of course with Ron not at work, there were no wages. He hadn't been there long enough to get any sick pay, so we had to make inroads on our precious savings.

One day there was a shout at the front door and Jimmy Bloom stood there with an enormous secondhand fridge in his arms. He brought it in and fixed it up in our little kitchen. He had an envelope which he handed to me.

It contained about ten pounds which had been collected from the men at work. I protested that I couldn't possibly accept the fridge or the money.

'Don't you worry, Katy gal,' he said in his broad Cockney accent, 'You take it, you can put something towards the fridge when your lad is well again. Poor bastard, we can't see him like this. Put some cold drink in here for him, it's as hot as hell in here. The fellas at work all send best wishes, tell him to get well soon.' He strode out to his truck and drove away. He was over six feet tall and weighed nearly twenty stone, was tremendously strong and could carry a full-sized fridge as if it were a parcel of groceries, but was one of the kindest people I had ever met. How grateful we were for that fridge. I made lemonade which Ron could manage to drink and the children, it seemed from the whole street, queued up for iced lollies!

Ron began to improve, the paralysis didn't set in, we were so lucky, but it was almost a month before he returned to work. He was very shaky but when I think of what the outcome might have been, I still shudder. The children went back to school and I decided to try once again to find a part-time job. Our savings had taken such a plunge during Ron's illness that I felt I must add something to them. We must have enough by June for the fare home, that was priority number one!

Chapter 19

The Last Lap

Mrs O'Malley worked harder than any person I have ever known. She went out before five o'clock in the morning to an office cleaning job, returning soon after eight to hurry her children off to school. As soon as they had left she went to work as a cleaner in a lodging house for Italians which was nearby. At midday she would return for a snack, usually bringing with her as many as thirty shirts to wash. She would light the wood-burning copper in the outhouse we used as a laundry, and boil the clothes. The Italians were spotlessly clean, always wearing well pressed trousers and white shirts. The dry-cleaning shops did a roaring trade as the men had no facilities in their lodgings. In fact many of them lived entirely on the verandahs, using an iron bedstead and keeping their belongings in a suitcase under the bed. Mrs O'Malley charged them two shillings per shirt. As she hung them on the line they would dry so quickly that she would fill the line, then go back to the beginning again and take them in. This applied to us all, of course; the back garden was small and enclosed and the heat was intense. The sun took a toll from our clothes; dresses lasted only a few months and anything with a yellow pattern in the fabric would quickly wear out, disintegrating into small holes.

At five o'clock Mrs O'Malley would have left the house again to return the newly-ironed shirts and continue to the offices where she then started her evening shift. At around eight-thirty she would come wearily into the house and have a meal. It was the only time I ever saw her eat anything substantial. The family were no help to her at all. Mr O'Malley worked an ordinary eight-hour day, but never lifted a finger indoors, save for his one job. As the toilet was outside and there was no light in the garden they, like the rest of us, had to improvise if they needed to use a toilet in the night. The O'Malleys obviously hadn't got a bucket, for each morning as I went to the kitchen a horrible smell met my nostrils. The door to their second room was often ajar and there, in the middle of the floor, a large aluminium saucepan would be standing. It was always brimming over with urine and it would have a head of foam on it like a glass of Guinness, hanging over, waiting to drop.

Mr O'Malley would empty this most mornings, his wife already at work. I would watch with horrid fascination from my kitchen, as he tottered down the passage heading for the back door. He never made it without some spillage; he would get as far as the back door and give up. I never knew whether he ever intended to go as far as the toilet with his burden, but he certainly never did. Once at the back door he would just fling the contents up the patch of sand and go, grumbling, back indoors. I used to wait until he had gone to work and then, with rubber gloves, wash the passage floor with Dettol, to try and rid the house of smelling like a public lavatory!

Mrs O'Malley did very little cleaning indoors but considering the long hours she worked, it was no wonder. The family diet consisted of salad, corned beef and the occasional boiled potatoes. I admired her; she was determined to get her family back home and, knowing how hard it was for us to save our fares, I dreaded to think how much harder it was for her. Six fares to find, four of them being at full rate. She had a mammoth task ahead.

I started looking for a job but, wanting only part-time and that to fit in with taking Vivienne to and from school, it was almost impossible. Finally I found one, as an office cleaner, in the same block as Mrs O'Malley! So we would set off together in the mornings to walk into the city centre. At five a.m. we would pass the many lodging houses and see the rows of beds, their occupants fast asleep on the verandahs; some of the men would have rigged up pieces of rattan blinds to give a little privacy. How dirty the streets were at that hour of the morning: beer cans, chip packets, bottles and vomit in all the gutters, and often the perpetrators of the rubbish would be lying there too. What a difference when we returned after eight and the dustcarts and road sprays had been round.

At times the Catholic Church would ship out young single Italian girls as wives for these men, having been through a form of marriage in their home towns first. These shiploads were known as the 'proxy brides'. We were told that some of the girls had never met their 'husbands' until the ship docked at Fremantle. Not very far removed from the old West, and the 'mail order brides' we used to read about.

I found the office cleaning very hard work; the huge hand polishers for the enormous open-plan offices were heavy, and required some strength to move them. I was allocated a floor belonging to an oil company, whose workers were unbelievably untidy. One desk in particular was always littered with sweet papers, fruit peel and cigarette ash. The waste paper basket was invariably empty, the contents being strewn across the floor. There were sixty desks in that room and this one was always the worst. One day, when I arrived for the evening shift, the occupant had evidently had a bag of cherries, the evidence was all around. I picked up every cherry stone and after polishing the desk I wrote on it, in the stones, HAVE YOU EVER HEARD OF A WASTE PAPER BASKET? PLEASE USE IT. It worked, I never had any more trouble; for the rest of the time I worked there he or she was careful to leave the desk tidy. When I left the office in the morning I would meet Ron halfway to the city; he would have Vivienne with him, then I would take her straight on to school. In the evenings the position would be reversed, I would meet him on his way home, hand Vivienne over to him and continue on my way. My routine in the mornings never varied. After leaving her at school I would go back to the room, shower, change and have my breakfast. Then, three times a week, I would pack a few sandwiches and go to the cinema. It was cheap, but more important than that, it was cool!

All the cinemas were air-conditioned, what a relief. I would stay there until three o'clock, which meant I had seen the programme twice as they opened at ten in the morning. I have never sat through so many dreadful films, and a few good ones. Then I would go directly to St. Bridget's to fetch Vivienne. We would go back to our room for a wash and a cold drink before heading for the city and meeting Ron. I think five in the afternoon was the hottest time of the day; the heat that rose up from the pavements was just as if an oven door had been opened during a baking session. It literally stopped your breath. After work I used to drag my way home, soaked with sweat and so weary that it was an effort to walk, almost too tired to eat the meal Ron had prepared when I got in. But every few pounds that went into our savings was another turn of the screws, we said. I had to join the Union of course, before I was allowed to start work, and pay the year's subscription in advance, as was the practice. In fact, that took my first week's wages.

Ron loved his job at the electrical company. We have often wondered if that job had been available when we first went West whether things might have turned out differently. Ron worked mostly with Jimmy Bloom and we became quite friendly with him and his wife Nan. They had three sons, Keith, Mickey and Billy. Then some years after the boys they had produced a little girl, Beth, whom they all adored. Nan was as tiny as Jimmy was enormous, but she ruled them all with a firm hand. Those boys did as their mother told them, as did Jimmy, and they were beautifully behaved. Jimmy was the funniest person that Ron or I have ever met, before or since.

I had been warned before I met him about his bad language, at times absolutely obscene, but even then I hadn't been prepared for the expressions he used. No matter what he said, it was done in such a manner that you couldn't take offence. Neither Nan nor the children used a coarse word; they wouldn't have dared, Jimmy would have been furious with them. He was born of a Jewish father and an Irish mother and was a Catholic, like his children. Every Saturday night they would all go to confession and to early morning Mass on Sunday. This, Jimmy believed, absolved him from having to bother about his behaviour the rest of the week.

In spite of his size he was the most soft-hearted, sentimental person you could meet. One day when we arrived at his house he was sitting morosely in a corner. Nan was beside him. 'Whatever is the matter, Jimmy,' she asked.

'Oh, Nannie, gal,' he replied, 'I've just seen the most awful thing. I've just seen a blind man on the corner with no arms.'

Nan looked puzzled, 'That's dreadful for the poor man, but why are you so upset? There's nothing you can do.' she said.

'Nannie gal, what does the poor bastard do when he wants a piss?' His face was so mournful that we dared not laugh; he was being quite serious. When Ron was out with Jimmy on deliveries, if an elderly person or a child was trying to cross the road, Jimmy would stop the vehicle, get out and hold up his hand to halt all the traffic. He would see them safely across the road, oblivious of the hoots and rude gestures of the other drivers. On one unforgettable occasion, as they were driving through the main street of the city a bus drew alongside. The driver cleared his throat and spat out of his window, the mucus landed on the windscreen in front of Jimmy and trickled down the glass. He accelerated, caught the bus up, and swerved in front of it causing the driver to brake suddenly and stop. Jimmy climbed deliberately out of his van, walked up to the cab of the bus, opened the door and hauled the wretched driver out by the collar of his coat. He dragged him over to the van, rubbed his nose against the glass, thrust a rag into his hand and roared, 'Now clean it off, you dirty bastard!'

The bus driver obeyed meekly and scuttled back to his bus. Ron said the passengers were hanging out of the windows, open-mouthed, while half the traffic in Perth looked on. He said he sank low in the passenger seat, wishing he were elsewhere.

Any day or evening spent with Jimmy was one long laugh, although he didn't mean to be funny. We never knew what circumstances had driven him from home, but he certainly sailed very close to the wind in his wheelings and dealings when we knew him. He had a wicked sense of humour at times, as all his workmates found out. One of them was a young Italian who had only been in the country a short time and was trying hard to improve his English. He was given the most menial jobs in the stores and felt that when he had mastered the language he would be promoted. One day he said to Jimmy, 'Tell me, please. In Italy when we see someone go, we say "*Arrivederci*", what say here?'

Straight-faced Jimmy replied, 'Here, Gino, we say "Arseholes".' The lads thought this was a huge joke. If Gino had to answer the phone he would always say pleasantly before he rung off, 'Arseholes.' It ceased to be a joke the day the boss rang through to the stores with a message. Gino answered the phone, carefully repeated the message and with a cheerful 'Arseholes, Mr Thomassio,' put the phone down. Poor Gino, he was on the carpet in no time, but Jimmy owned up to being the culprit, and such was his personality that the boss took it in good part, and Gino was let off. Gino was also the cause of much amusement over another incident. He was a very handsome young man with dark curly hair and twinkling brown eyes. He was single but had a girlfriend back in his native Naples, whom he hoped to go home to and bring back as his bride when he had saved enough money.

Like many Italians he was very fond of his family and longed for the day when he would have a home and children of his own. This did not prevent him, however, taking the occasional trip to Roe Street. Usually this would be on a Saturday night when, in company with some other young Italian lads, he would enjoy a few beers and round off the evening with a visit to one of the brothels. On the Monday mornings he would regale his workmates with tales of his exploits which, delivered in his broken English, were looked forward to with relish as it was always good for a laugh.

He usually patronised the same brothel as he was attracted to a girl that worked there. She was Eurasian, very slim, with enormous dark eyes and an enchanting smile. Although he only called about once a month, each time he asked for Nina, as she was called, but he had never been lucky as she was always with a client or awaiting one by appointment. He became quite obsessive about it and one Monday morning when he arrived at work was obviously bursting with news. Such remarks as, 'Looks as if Gino had been lucky at last,' or 'What put the sparkle in your eyes, sport?' brought no response. He was not saying a word until he had all their attention. During the mid-morning break he came into the staff room, sat down and in his dramatic fashion said, 'Fellas, I must tell you that on Saturday night I was robbed!'

He waited for them all to be quiet and began his tale. 'I meet the boys, we have a few beers, like always, then we go to Roe Street, I am needing a leedle affection, yes? I wait my turn, just sitting, patient. She is there, this Nina, I tell you, she ees so bootiful. Those eyes and the way she smile. She ees no such busy this time, I see that, and the madam, she say I can have her! Think on that, so many times I have asked and, tonight, she ees mine! We go to her room and she had the music playing. It ees the one they play all times on the radio, "Softly, Softly". This woman Ruby Murray I think.' (It was the big hit in England at that time.) 'I say to mine self, this night is my lucky one, the dreamy song, so slow, so soft. She gets ready and I too, I so hurried, I am, how you say, in passion? I sit down on the bed and she walk over to me, then she stop and put one other record on. Call it "Bimbo, Bimbo", you know? It go so fast, like a man gallop a horse. She say to me, "You work to this one please." In five minutes I am at the door, five minutes! Then she say I pay ten pounds, ten pounds! I never pay ten pounds before! I was robbed. For this much money I could speak to my Maria on a telephone, oh, it ees a sin!' He beat his brow and looked so mournful; needless to say there was no sympathy from his workmates, they all thought it hilarious and he never lived it down.

Whenever I hear 'Softly, Softly' or 'Bimbo' played on the radio today, and both records are still played quite often, I think of Ron telling me Gino's tale. I wonder if he ever did go back to Naples and return with his Maria, as his bride.

That summer was, like the previous one, breaking all records for heat, and the children were outdoors as soon as they came home from school. Jimmy had delivered a huge crate to the house, for Ron to break up and build a packing case strong enough to transport our fridge home. No one we knew owned such an object at the time in England, so we decided to take ours with us. Today, it would be unusual to find a home without one! This crate became the source of all the children's games. Kenny O'Malley invented the most imaginative pastimes for the entire street. Children of every nationality would gather in the sandy back garden on Saturdays or in the evenings, and wait for Kenny to organise them.

The crate could be a ship, a concert platform, a train or bus, or, their favourite, the altar of a church. He would drape it in a not very clean sheet, place candles at either end, a rough cross in the middle and conduct a service, dressed in a long white shirt of his father's with the collar turned back to front. Raspberry cordial would be the holy wine and small squares of bread the holy wafers. I know it sounds blasphemous but these children of all religions and races, sometimes twenty in number, would sit in rows, all partaking of Kenny's 'Holy Communion'. His sermons were given in a curious mixture of Italian and English, with odd words of Polish and Greek thrown in for good measure. We used to watch and listen, hidden in our kitchen, trying to stifle our amusement; we felt sure that Kenny was destined to become a great entertainer. Vivienne has never forgotten those games and still talks about them today. It seemed a shame when a few weeks before we were due to sail Ron had to dismantle the crate and restructure it to fit the fridge.

We saw very little of the Thornes or Mrs Tanner. The Thornes were out at work all day, and Mrs Tanner kept herself to herself. In April she went away for a weekend to an old friend, whom we had met once or twice; Miss Hogben was the only caller she ever had. We knew that Mrs Tanner's son lived not far away but I don't think he saw his mother often. On the Monday, Mrs Tanner returned; she spoke to us briefly and, saying she had a headache, went to her room. We hadn't seen her at all the rest of the day and about nine in the evening we heard a crash and ran to see what was amiss. She was lying on the floor, foaming at the mouth. It appeared that she had suffered a stroke. Ron ran to the nearest phone box to call an ambulance while Mrs O'Malley and I tried to help her. It seemed ages before the ambulance arrived, by which time she was deeply unconscious. She was placed on a stretcher and the two men lifted her but, as they were taking her out of the door, one of the men lost his hold on the handles and dropped the stretcher. She crashed to the floor and we watched, horrified, as they hastily picked her up, not gently, and hurried her off in the ambulance.

The Thornes were out for the evening and Mrs O'Malley and I cleaned up the room and stripped her bed, quite sure that we would never see her again. She died that same night and Mary notified her son, who seemed totally unmoved, the funeral was hurriedly arranged and her few belongings removed. Les and Mary, who had known her for several years, were very upset; they felt that Donald Tanner wanted everything over so quickly, as if his mother's life had never been. So the room was to let once more.

Two days later there was a knock at the open front door. To our surprise it was Bill and Sally Van Dyck. They had written to Korrine to ask how we were and the letter had been returned so they guessed we had left. Sally had then thought to write to Len who had told her our new address. It was lovely to see them but they were in trouble. Their job had come to an end so they had returned to Perth but were jobless and homeless. They were seeking work and afraid to touch their savings lest there wouldn't be enough for the passage to Holland, which they had booked for September. Could we help them, they wondered?

Mrs Tanner's death in one way did help them. We smuggled them into her room; it was only a single bed but they could manage, and they didn't pay any rent as the agent wasn't due for almost two weeks. We had to tell the other occupants of the house though, but we all agreed it would give them a breathing space and perhaps they would be lucky enough to find jobs by then and could take over the room legitimately. They ate their meals with us and every day went out seeking work. The day the agent called for the rent we told him the room still hadn't been let, having first removed all traces of their presence. Dishonest I suppose, but we paid enough between us for very little convenience.

At the end of three weeks they were still jobless. That evening Bill sat at our table, sank his head in his hands and wept. It was an awful sight, to see a big man like Bill, who had fought with the Resistance movement and faced terrible dangers, brought so low by unemployment. During the fourth week, when they knew the agent would soon be calling again, in sheer desperation, they took another joint post, hundreds of miles north, in a bush hotel. We went with them to the railway station, promising to keep in touch and giving them my mother's address so they could contact us back home.

Our time was running out, months had become weeks and weeks days. Ron was working his notice out when his boss came to see me one afternoon. He was a dour Scotsman and he pleaded with me to stay. 'Don't go, Mrs Upton, I'm sure you are making a big mistake. Ron is a good worker, we all want him to stay. In a few months he'll get a promotion and could be posted to Melbourne or Sydney. Go home for a holiday with your wee lassie, see your folk, then you'll probably want to come back.'

I said, 'It was a joint decision that we should go, but if Ron really wants to stay, then I am quite willing to go home for a holiday as you suggest. You talk it over with him.'

This he did, at great length, apparently, but Ron was adamant, we must go together. So the time for departure drew close and we began to say our goodbyes. We spent a Sunday seeing all our neighbours from Tinton, the Shales, the Mounts and Caseys. Alan, May and the children were coming down to the docks to see us off but we had a last meal at their home. We went to see Len's parents, who were actually sailing the week before us to visit England, the first time that Edward had been home since he left as a boy of sixteen. They were going to stay for three months or so, visiting the many relations who still lived in Sussex, and Scotland to see a cousin of Wilma's father.

Frank and Jean and the family would be at the docks also. Their own date was drawing near and they would follow us in a couple of months. We were to spend the last night with Jimmy and Nan as they had room for us to sleep at their house. Our luggage had to be at the dock on the Saturday so we hired a truck to pick up our boxes, the Dutch trunk and the crate containing our precious fridge. Only our personal luggage would be going with us in our cabins. By teatime our room had been cleaned, all our clothes packed, nothing left to do but bid goodbye to the O'Malleys and the Thornes. They crowded out onto the verandah to see us off, Jimmy arrived in his big old Ford and we loaded up. We drove away from New Street, waving until we turned the corner and the shabby old house was out of sight. I felt like I had when we had left Albion Road in Brisbane, quite sad. It isn't where you live that is important, it is the people around you. Although New Street was in such an awful district I was happier there than anywhere else in Australia.

We had a merry meal that night with Jimmy and Nan; she had cooked some lovely dishes for us. As we were eating, their eldest son, Keith, came in. He had left school recently and had obtained his first job, in a hardware store. He was smiling broadly, greeted us, and, bursting with pride, handed Nan his first wage packet. 'For you, mum,' he said, as if it were a gift of precious jewels. He went off to have a shower. Jimmy beamed.

'Nannie gal, did you see his face, DID YOU SEE HIS FACE?' He emphasised the words. 'Oh, he was as pleased as a prostitute with two fannies!'

How we laughed; same old Jimmy, it was fitting that our last evening together should end on such a laugh!

The next morning we left for the docks and the *Arcadia*, the flagship of the P&O fleet. It was the Captain's last voyage as he was about to retire and, although we didn't know it then, he was to make it a sentimental journey, taking the ship off its route, to visit some little island or port that wasn't on the schedule, to say his own farewells. This made it a memorable voyage for all on board. We seemed to have a lot of friends at the docks; everyone came aboard for the last hour, and then as we ourselves had done on so many occasions, said goodbye. Hugs, kisses and tears as we watched them file down the gangplank. We lined the rails with the hundreds of fellow travellers, holding our coloured streamers as the band played the same old tunes: 'Now is the hour', 'Life on the ocean wave' and finally, 'Anchors aweigh'. Frank, Jean and the children, Jimmy, Nan, May and Alan all caught our streamers, holding on tightly, calling out, 'Take care', 'Promise you'll write', 'Give my love to Blighty' and so on and Jean's voice at the last, floating over the water, 'We'll see you soon, only a few months now.'

The *Arcadia* pulled away from the quay, the coloured ribbons broke and drifted on to the ripples as we steamed toward the open sea. It was over, the long voyage had begun, and we were going home!

Epilogue

We have kept in touch with some of the people we met during our travels in Australia. Joy and Phillip eventually moved from their smallholding and created a beautiful nursery garden, not far from Hastings. They were well known throughout the area until they retired a few years ago. They had a house built on their own land and still live among the trees and shrubs that once formed part of their business. We often meet and share our many memories.

Fred and Kate stayed in Queensland and, after almost twenty years, returned to their old neighbourhood in Essex. Kate settled very well but not Fred. He missed the hot climate, the very thing that had caused so much ill health and discomfort to Kate. We spent several weeks together when they stayed at our house; both were nearing eighty then and were undecided as to their best course of action. Several of their sons were still in Australia; only the daughter with whom they were staying had remained in England. Finally they went back to Queensland and we only had one letter. Kate had been involved in a serious car accident and was not making a good recovery. The daughter in Essex had moved away and we were unable to trace her, so we lost touch entirely. It is unlikely that Fred or Kate are sill alive, but we remember them with affection.

Of all the family who shared our lives in Albion Road, only Hans and Corrie are still part of it. We visit each other in turn. They live in the bungalow they built when they returned to Holland. It is in a pleasant village in the east of the country and, in spite of the years between, they seem hardly changed at all.

We heard that Mrs Shale died soon after we came home, and although we never corresponded with Will we believe that he died some years ago. Jack and Janey Mount moved across country to Melbourne about the time we sailed and we lost touch, and if the Caseys are still around they would be in their nineties! Knowing how strong Jonnie was, it is possible.

I still write to May; sadly, Alan died while only in his forties. May came to England for a visit several years ago; she was just the same, cheerful, practical and with the same sense of humour. When we met we both shrieked, 'You haven't changed a bit!' She only visited us the once as her time was so limited but it was great to see her. Her family are all married and she has about seven grandchildren. Now there are none of her relatives left over here it is unlikely that she will make another trip.

Derek and Maureen Greenfield live in the Midlands and we meet every year. The little baby who used to sleep on the edge of the mattress while we ate our meals with them, is now a mature student at Sydney University. He returned to the land of his birth three years ago. Whether he will remain there after he has completed his course remains to be seen.

Frank, Jean and family lived in London until five years ago, when Frank retired. They moved to Wiltshire, followed a year or so later by both their daughters and Colin. The girls are married as is the eldest son, James. He now lives in Australia, having moved there after the tragic death of his eldest son. He and his wife decided to make a new life out there, but did come back on holiday last year.

We never kept in touch with any of the New Street folk, but we know that the O'Malleys did manage to save enough money for the voyage. Jean had one letter from them after she and Frank were back in London. I was pleased that Mrs O'Malley got her desire; she certainly earned it.

Somehow we lost touch with Jimmy and Nan. We exchanged letters at first, then it dwindled to Christmas cards, they moved once or twice and the correspondence stopped altogether. Ron swears that he once saw Jimmy on the television, sitting in the front row of a London theatre, laughing his head off at the antics of a well known comedian! He shouted to me, 'Look, there's Jimmy Bloom! Look, there.' But I was too late, the camera had moved on. We have often wondered though if they did return.

Bill and Sally wrote once or twice, after we returned. They did go home and Bill was working in the docks at Rotterdam. Sally found it difficult to write in English and, like Jimmy and Nan, after a while there were no more answers to our letters. We hope all is well with them and that they made a good life back in their own country.

Edward and Wilma visited us a number of times. They were frequent visitors to Sussex, and indeed to many other counties, between them having a large family of cousins in this country. We used to look forward to their visits. They always stayed several months and we would meet them whenever we could. Wilma hasn't been since Edward died three years ago, but we hope she might come again sometime. Len, her son, who used to eat in our kitchen at Korrine, has been over twice in recent years. He and his wife visit us; he has become a very successful farmer and has a large property in West Australia, with two sons also involved in the farms.

We are saving now to go back and spend a holiday out there, retracing our steps, from East to West, and, hopefully, visiting all our old haunts. We feel we may be able to trace some of our old companions through the pages of the telephone book. I know it is impossible to correspond with all the people we knew, but we don't forget them. What a sentimental journey it will be when we return! We have never had any regrets about our far wanderings, or that we came back. In spite of some hard times and near poverty we had a lot of fun and some wonderful experiences. I feel, like Hilaire Belloc:

> From quiet homes and first beginnings
> Out to the undiscovered ends,
> There's nothing worth the wear of winning
> But laughter and the love of friends.